John Ashford/Peter Willett

Text Retrieval and Document Databases

Studentlitteratur   Chartwell-Bratt

British Library Cataloguing in Publication Data
Ashford, J. H. (John Hatfield), *1933-*
    Text Retrieval and Document Databases
    1. On-line computer systems. Machine-readable files
    I. Title II. Willett, Peter, *1953-*
    005.74
ISBN 0-86238-204-1

© J Ashford, P Willett and Chartwell-Bratt Ltd, 1988

Chartwell-Bratt (Publishing and Training) Ltd
ISBN 0-86238-204-1

Printed in Sweden,
Studentlitteratur, Lund

ISBN 91-44-29571-5   1 2 3 4 5 6 7 8 9 10 | 1992 91 90 89

Preface

This book is intended to provide a general, easily accessible account of text databases, and of the ways in which this basic technology is being applied and diversified into text + data, text + image and others as *document databases.* It is written to appeal to students of computing science, information science and librarianship, but also to be of value to computer managers and systems analysts dealing with office automation and document management projects, and to users planning to get the best from their Computer Departments.

Chapters 1, 3, 5, 7 and 14 are adapted and extended from a series of articles in Computer News in the summer of 1988. With chapters 2 and 6, which are intended to give a flavour of systems in use, they cover the established nucleus of the subject. Chapters 4 and 8 deal with technical aspects of design, mainly on the text side, and might be omitted on a first reading. Chapters 9 to 13 cover applications of optical disc storage and special purpose hardware, and identify research and development topics which we believe are likely to lead to new developments. Finally, chapter 14 offers a basis for system evaluation and selection.

No attempt has been made to deal with the on-line bibliographic services and data vendors such as DIALOG, ORBIT or BRS in detail. These are specialised electronic publishing systems, and although they share the same text retrieval technology, it is a relatively small part of their data gathering, distribution and charging operations. They have also been much written about elsewhere (Hall, 1986; Gilreath, 1984; Staud, 1988; and the Proceedings of the Online Information Meetings). Nor have we attempted to deal with library automation *per se,* although the subject matter of this book is clearly relevant to librarians moving from the custodial era to that of the computer based information centre (Lovecy, 1984; Tedd, 1984). Readers who wish to follow up relational database technology are recommended to Oxborrow, 1986.

Chapter 15 contains a summary of the main sources of further information, especially in the journal literature, and together with the references should provide for those who wish to pursue the subjects of the book in more depth.

Acknowledgements

Computer News agreed that the summer 1988 articles *(Text Information Management Systems)* should be re-used, and Paul Breeze, their Features Editor helped to make them more readable. Aslib and authors granted permission to adapt figures 3.4 and 7.2 to 7.5 from articles in **Program**. Dr A S Pollitt kindly allowed us to adapt figures 11.1 to 11.5 from his PhD thesis. Material on INSTRUCT in chapter 10 is adapted, with permission, from Willett, Peter (ed.) *Document retrieval systems. (Volume 3, the Foundations of Information Science, ed. Blaise Cronin).* London: Taylor Graham, 1988 ISBN 0947568 21 2.

Many people from the text database developers helped when first the articles, and later the book were being written, and we wish to thank Michelle Durban and John Townsend (Information Dimensions); Robin Clough (Associated Knowledge Systems); Henry Cochran (Henco Software Inc.); Michael Hare (Doric Computer Systems); Jan Hultgren (Paralog (UK) Ltd.); Derek Matkin (Harwell Computer Power Ltd.); and Graham Seddon (BRS Europe). They provided examples, shared market research, discussed their development plans and argued constructively about some of the conclusions - all of great value.

Olwen Terris produced the index, and improved the accuracy of the English and the intelligibility of the text. Any remaining errors are the authors'!

JA & PW

Production note

Since desk top publishing is a hot topic in 1988, and will probably still be of interest for a while - here is how this book was made. The original text of Chapters 1-9, 14, and all preliminary matter was set using MacAuthor (also known as LaserAuthor) version 1.4, and later MacAuthor II, on a Macintosh Plus micro computer with 1 Mb of memory and a 20Mb Qisk hard disc. Chapters 10-13 were first prepared on a Prime system using the local page editor and spelling checker, and the text was transferred through KERMIT to a Macintosh 3.5 inch floppy disc by Sheffield University Computing Services Department. This text was read in to MacAuthor II as an ASCII file, and reformatted. COACH was used as an on-line spelling checker, but the better, if occasionally fallible, hyphenation option in MacAuthor was preferred.

The figures were produced in MacDraw version 1.9.5 (and later MacDraw II), and pasted into frames within the MacAuthor text. No real difficulties were found in upgrading either software product in mid-stream. Footnotes became practical with MacAuthor II, and so were used both for occasional comments, and to include a limited glossary of technical terms as they occurred in the text. The cover was set separately by Chartwell-Bratt.

The Index was initially generated using the *index style* facility in MacAuthor, which allows selected terms and phrases to be invisibly marked. Thereafter, the individual chapters were built into a document stack using the Document Manager utility in MacAuthor, and HyperCard. A stack process option renumbered the pages in a single sequence, and Document Manager then scanned the paginated text and transferred the index terms and their page numbers to a sorted text-only file. This file was read back into MacAuthor for editing as the book index. Unfortunately, it was full of 'false drops' and redundant references, and not at all easy to use, and so was replaced - and very much improved - by Olwen Terris, using more traditional methods (see also chapter 10).

Camera ready copy was printed on a 300 dots per inch Apple LaserWriter SC (non-PostScript) printer, and reduced by approximately 75% to make the final printed pages. The founts are Macintosh standard laser printer Times (mostly 14 on 15pt. before reduction) and Helvetica for headings.

COACH is a trademark of Deneba Systems Inc.

HyperCard, LaserWriter, Macintosh and MacDraw are trademarks of Apple Computer Inc.

MacAuthor and Document Manager are software products of Icon Technology Limited, Leicester, UK

Contents

1 Introduction

Most computer programs deal with numeric or encoded information such as commercial data; scientific data; spatial data for air traffic control and weather forecasting; graphic data for computer-aided design. A substantial minority includes word processors, electronic mail and bulletin board systems, and it is a regular criticism that the era of the 'electronic office' has served merely to make more paper, faster! A few systems, maybe four or five thousand in all compared with the hundreds of thousands of general computing applications, deal with information in textual form as a resource, available for searching, selection, transmission, and eventually archiving.

Traditional computing systems store data, and then manipulate it by program to provide information. In this book we deal with the wider case, *total information management,* where information itself is stored and retrieved, in the form of documents, with words and numbers, drawings and pictures. Conventional data processing is included, through the use of gateways to other software.

The volume of published text is now huge. More than 420,000 new books are released each year in English and other European languages, by about ten thousand commercial publishers. There are at least 100,000 journals in the same languages, containing typically 50 or more articles each year. Add to these the non-commercial publications, the internal technical, administrative and operational papers of government and industrial organisations, and the great importance of textual material becomes apparent.

Why, then, have text management applications formed so small a part of the general data processing scene? And why, now, are they growing at a rate predicted by several researchers to exceed 60% per year for several years? Part of the reason has been the decreasing cost of the relatively large storage needed for text. Many commercial database applications, with a dozen or more users, fit into ten million characters (10Mb) of disc storage or less. 'Large', for numeric databases, seems to begin at about 50 Mb. Ten million characters, representing 3,500 to 4,000 A4 (or quarto) pages from a word processor, is less than a year's output from a fluent typist, and text databases in the 100 Mb region are normal. The rapid reduction in the real cost of magnetic disc storage in the last four years, and the promised further gains with erasable optical discs have very much reduced the problems of storing large volumes of text - but still the word processors turn out paper for filing in cabinets, and the electronic record is kept only so long as it is needed for editing and revision!

The second challenge for text, or natural language, processing has been the apparent lack of structure. Now, although it is indeed difficult to make text and images fit into fixed length boxes and behave like COBOL[1] data files, there are two real and useful structures available in natural language.

One structure is the subdivision of both spoken and written language into words and the collection of the words into sentences. A native speaker of a language, or one who has become genuinely fluent, hardly has to think about this level of subdivision, but separates out and interprets the elements with ease. For computing purposes, the separation of written text by spaces in most European languages, and of characters in ideographic texts (Chinese, Japanese, Korean) provides a good starting point. Text management systems deal with the **form** of language, that is, the strings of characters comprising the text, and not directly with its meaning, and just how they treat punctuation, and how connexions with meaning may be made will be discussed in later chapters.

Written (or better, typed, or word processed) texts usually have a second level of structure at document level, which may be applied in particular text databases. Common examples are author, title, abstract, section, in technical reports; or sender, destination, subject, date, paragraph, action required, in electronic mail memoranda. What the information management system must then do, is to deal efficiently with the storage of variable length, unpredictable text streams, and at the same time hold structural and indexing data in fixed formats to allow fast, and not too complex processing, both in retrieval from databases, and, especially, in updating in large systems. With the widespread use of word processing equipment, large volumes of text are already available in a suitable format.

The third difficulty, which has often caused delays in acceptance of text management systems in traditional computer departments, is that text retrieval is inherently probabilistic and, in contrast with data retrieval (eg. 'find all staff with salaries > $18,000'), lacks absolute answers to searches. In text retrieval there is always a trade-off between having high *recall* in a search, and risking too large a results list, with many possible responses to be inspected and discarded - and looking for high *precision*, when all the results delivered are relevant, but some desirable records are missed because of the narrower search profiles. The achievement of **both** high recall **and** high precision is a popular target for information science research, but may in fact be not only pragmatically but also theoretically unachievable. This is a familiar topic for the *information scientist*, but is often found disturbing by data processing staff with a conventional *computer science* background, since complete recall **and** precision are easily obtained in *data* retrieval systems.

---

[1]   COBOL : a widely used, business directed, programming language.

The final, and until recently the really intractable problem area, has been that real documents contain not only text, but line drawings, tables, and pictures of the subjects to which they relate, sometimes in black and white, but often in colour. *Geographic information systems,* which have been slowly maturing over the last decade, are now flourishing as the potential for representing spatial data in tabular, textual **and** graphical form is realised. In the first four chapters, the emphasis is on the text storage and retrieval requirements - later chapters deal with the new methods being applied to 'complete information parcels', and from chapter 9 onwards new hardware[1] approaches and research and development initiatives.

The 'text' part is well known

The major text database systems date from the early 1970s. One strand of development was from computer typesetting of indexes to published journals in science and medicine (the so-called 'secondary journals') to storing the same texts in electronic form in on-line 'dial up[2]' host systems. Projects by Lockheed for NASA (RECON) and by Systems Development Corporation for the National Library of Medicine, Washington (ELHILL) were the first steps towards the DIALOG and ORBIT services respectively. These now support hundreds of bibliographic files, and thousands of subscribers.

In parallel, but with a good deal of common technology, AERE Harwell, Battelle Laboratories in Columbus, Ohio, and IBM built text database systems for their own purposes - which became STATUS, BASIS and STAIRS respectively. AERE and IBM were originally most interested in the full text of statutes and other legal documents, Battelle in internal databases of technical information. In an interesting 'hybrid' case, BRS Information Technologies established an on-line host business using IBM STAIRS, then developed their own package to improve both storage and response performance, finally marketing it as an independent software product, BRS/SEARCH. Several other packages were developed in the early days of the minicomputer, and some have survived on a small scale, while the availability of super-micros has yet again stimulated a number of developments. Since 1975, however, although IBM STAIRS development appears to have been very limited, BASIS, BRS/SEARCH and STATUS have evolved continuously, and now share the major part of all markets except IBM mainframes. Here STAIRS is still widely installed, though now under increasing competitive pressure, and is believed to have over 1,200 active sites among nearly 2,000 licences[3].

The on-line host systems, 'data vendors' or, as they are often called now, 'spinners', have increasingly made use of special purpose software to deal

---

[1] hardware : the tangible parts of a computer system; cf software.

[2] dial up : a form of on-line access by public telephone network. On-line is used in this book in the sense of a continuous interaction with a computer system.

[3] IBM does not usually provide such data, so these figures are 'IBM watchers' guesses'.

with problems of large scale remote enquiry and its associated billing. Although for some years they were offered for sale as 'in-house' packages as well as being used in their data vendor rôles, now only BRS/SEARCH has a 'top five' position in both markets. The specialised subject of the on-line data services is not covered in this book, except so far as they share text management methodology with the 'in-house' software products, but a good account of both the major systems and the bibliographic databases on offer will be found in Hall (1986). Discussion of the on-line full text and financial data markets, and an extensive bibliography will be found in AGARD (1986), and an analytical study in Staud (1988).

System structure

Most established systems have the same major components, although the way in which they are integrated varies (Figure 1.1). All must have some

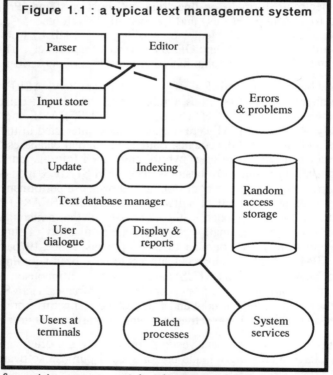

Figure 1.1 : a typical text management system

means of acquiring new material, selecting useful words from the text, and building indexes and a cumulative text file. This is called the 'parser' stage. An editor is needed, both to work with the new text before updating[1], and to

---

[1] update : to select a record, change it, and replace it, re-indexing if necessary.

maintain the text within the database itself. In some systems, when text is derived directly from a word processor, that word processor itself may be used as an optional editor for the stored text. The main modules of the text management system proper are the update processor, the text indexing system (or 'inverted file processor'), the user dialogue handler, and, usually, an interface for batch processes and output report processing. The system services gateway is where many of the new graphics and image applications are interfaced, and would also be the likely route for communication with conventional data processing systems when manipulation of numeric data is part of the total information requirement.

Text management in practice

Although management of full text of documents was an important objective of the designers of early text database systems, and the on-line legal systems have always offered full text, the principal application before 1983 was the storage and retrieval of bibliographic data. This comprised either catalogue records for in-house libraries of books and journals, or references to techni-

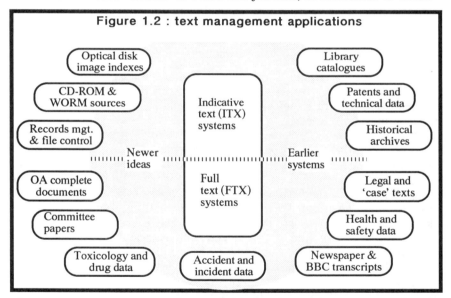

Figure 1.2 : text management applications

cal reports, papers, patents and so on held elsewhere. These are typical indicative text applications (ITX), where the use of the text database is to identify and point to documents held elsewhere, on paper, on microfilm, or, of more interest now, on optical disc as page images.

Since about 1983, the reduction in cost of disc[1] storage, and the availability of large volumes of text from office automation applications have shifted the

---

[1] disc : when used unqualified = magnetic disc storage device; some prefer disk.

balance towards full text (FTX) storage of complete documents - news transcripts, legal texts, office papers and technical data sheets.

The user within the organisation has changed also. When bibliographic applications predominated, the stimulus to acquire text management systems often came from librarians and information officers, some already familiar with the on-line data vendors. Some systems, in fact, were installed as independent minicomputer installations because computer departments 'did not want to know', and the library went ahead on its own initiative. More recently, the end user has been a committee secretary, a toxicologist or a practising lawyer, and the service, while still strongly user oriented, has been based on a computer centre facility. Central control of buying of office equipment, as local word processing evolved into networks, has also increased the involvement of data processing (DP) staff in text systems.

The scope of both full text and indicative text applications is shown in Figure 1.2. This represents the necessary foundation of natural language information systems upon which the later, hybrid databases of text, vector drawings and raster images have been constructed. For the venturesome, it may be of interest that, given suitable equipment and software for input and output of characters, this diagram applies equally well to information systems in character texts, and in fact the first copy of Chinese + English STATUS on Wang equipment has been delivered in Taiwan.

There are, being realistic, some bounds to the 'total information system' argument! Total information management systems are not going to be used for real time control systems; or for high volume transaction processing[1] (except maybe in special 'read only' contexts); or for purely numeric computing such as matrix processing. Less obviously, there are some text related projects where the scope of a total information management processor is useful, but not essential. They include document retrieval from archives using a few fixed field keys; profile search for word processor documents using sequential string search, and so on. It has been observed in office automation studies (Ashford, 1987a) that about one half of all office automation documents have lives of less than six months, and are best kept in temporary 'electronic heaps' or 'file & folder' conventions, searchable on their headings, or by standard word processor string matching. Such simple systems work well for small volumes, and have a place in office automation in particular. Above 10 million characters of stored text however, the real text processors become not only desirable, but essential.

In particular, if an application must be equally accessible and flexible at corporate, departmental and individual level; if it involves adaptation to a 'vertical' requirement with application specific user interfaces and reports as are needed for medical information, or police records of serious crimes, or risk assessment databases; if the same system must run on mainframe, mini-

---

[1]   transaction processing : like travel reservation systems, bank cash machines.

computer and micro computers for these users, then a product with a considerable investment in software, technical support, documentation and training is likely to be the only satisfactory solution.

Figure 1.3 summarizes the main groups of organisation where total information management systems are found, and typical applications for each class of user. Figure 1.4 shows the major text retrieval software package products.

Figure 1.3 : Who uses text based systems. . . and what for?

a) Government & manufacturing industry

Committee minutes	Chamber proceedings	Full text
Safety regulations	Standards	
Legal texts & contracts	Public enquiries	
Competitor data	Technical reports	
'Electronic archives' from office automation systems		

Land & property data	Project documentation	Structured
Software fault analysis	Police & security records	texts
Patents and data sheets	Research management systems	

Library catalogues	Archive management	Indicative
Maps & drawings indexes	Assets records	Texts

b) . . . . and among the service providers

Technical documentation	On-line textbooks	Full text
Market research data	Medical bulletins	
News & cuttings services	Minutes and reports	
Public 'advice' services	Litigation support systems	
Environmental protection data	Client profiles and contacts	
'Electronic archives' from office automation systems		

Museum catalogues	Computer program libraries	Structured
Company accounts & reports	Experimental data	'texts'
Databases of hazardous chemicals, their handling, and emergency treatment		

Bibliographic databases	Catalogues of all sorts	Indicative
Professional staff data	Videodisc publications	texts
Personal research indexes	'Back issues' of journals	

....and, of course, many of those listed under Government & Industry!

The traditional users of text storage and retrieval systems were the librarian and information specialists in research, technical and medical libraries. In the last three years, other categories have grown rapidly to over 70% of recorded applications.

Figure 1.4 : The main text retrieval package products

There are more than one hundred package systems on the market, from main-frames to micro computers, which claim 'text retrieval' as their main application. An extensive listing will be found in Kimberley (1988). Of these products, only a few have significant market shares, and even fewer offer access to either database or image handling as well as to text information. The following data (for mid-1988) are believed to be reasonably sound, but should be treated with caution as the market is expanding rapidly, and competition is fairly severe. All these products have at least good text capability, and most of the 'majors' have database and image links also.

World-wide : mainframes & minicomputers

The main vendors, sharing more than 80% by value, are, alphabetically :

*   BRS Information Technologies

    BRS/SEARCH - Assembler version for IBM mainframes with MVS; 'C' language systems under UNIX; IBM under VM/CMS; DEC VAX under VMS; DG (AOS) and WANG (VS)

*   Harwell Computer Power (UK) and Computer Power (Australia, USA)

    STATUS - IBM, ICL, Honeywell-Bull and other mainframes; DEC VAX, DG, PRIME, Wang (VS) and other minis; UNIX based systems

*   Henco Software Inc (USA) and Doric Computer Systems (UK)

    INFOText and **INFO-DB+** - DEC VAX, PRIME, other minis.§

*   IBM (offices world wide)

    STAIRS - IBM 370 series under MVS & VM/CMS

*   Infodata Systems Inc (USA) and Software Engineering (Netherlands)

    INQUIRE - IBM mainframes under MVS or VM/CMS §

*   Information Dimensions Inc.

    BASIS - IBM, CDC and other mainframes; DEC VAX, Wang (VS) and other minicomputers; UNIX based machines

    DM - DEC VAX minicomputers; (IBM mainframe system due for release in 1988) §

(continued)

Figure 1.4   (continued)

World-wide : micro computers

Of the major mainframe and minicomputer systems, BRS/SEARCH and STATUS are significant also in the micro computer market. Among many small volume products, there appears to be at least one other leader on micro computers only :

* Zylab Corporation (USA) and Primary Process Software (UK)

   Zy Index - IBM compatibles and other MS-DOS systems; Intel 8088, 8086 and 80286

The somewhat elusive FULCRUM retrieval software, usually available only as an OEM component of special purpose retrieval systems, has now been 'packaged' for UNIX and MS-DOS systems by Laticorp Inc. and is marketed under the names of CONTEXT and (later version) TEXTBASE. The vendor claims large penetration of the North American market, and a foothold in Europe.

European based products

The following mainframe / minicomputer products are significant in Europe, although there is little data on their overall market status :

   ASSASSIN (IBM and ICL mainframe; DEC VAX) Associated Knowledge Systems, Stockton-on-Tees

   GOLEM (Siemens computers) Siemens AG, Munich

   MIMER IR (IBM mainframe; DEC VAX, Prime) Mimer Software AB, Uppsala §

   MISTRAL (Honeywell-Bull computers) Honeywell-Bull, Paris

   TRIP (DEC VAX) Paralog AB, Stockholm and Paralog (UK) Ltd, London

§   indicates DBMS (Database Management Systems) or R.DBMS (Relational DBMS) plus text

2 First session: basic dialogue

This chapter contains a brief sample of interactive dialogue with a small database of correspondence to illustrate the sort of interface which a user might expect to encounter in a fairly typical 'command driven' system. It uses the European Common Command Language (CCL), and also serves for comparison with chapter 6 where the same database is accessed through the DEC VAX All-in-One interface, as an example of 'page mode' interactions.

The software package used in the examples - which are adapted from the Training Manuals - is the TRIP software developed and marketed by Paralog AB (Stockholm) and Paralog (UK) Ltd, for use on DEC VAX equipment. It is distinctive in its awareness of the problems of diverse European languages, and also in having for some years applied methods based on research in information science in its indexing and retrieval structures.

The demonstration database - named CORR - contains letters and telexes, and each document constitutes a single record containing the text of the message, the category (letter or telex), date, and the names, addresses and countries of the senders and receivers. It is laid out in an internal structure like this :

Field name	Data type	Content	
rname	phrase	receiver :	name
rcomp	"	"	company
raddr	"	"	address
rcountry	"	"	country
sname	phrase	sender :	name
scomp	"	"	company
saddr	"	"	address
scountry	"	"	country
day	date	date of the message	
cat	phrase	type of communication	
content	text	text of the message	

Accessing the database

The first steps are to :

- Start TRIP   (local code)
- Enter your user name   (user data)
- Enter the user password   (private)
- RETURN or ENTER (calls SEARCH session)

This produces the basic TRIP CCL 'search screen' like this :

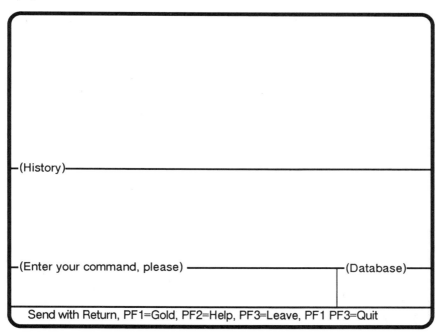

```
┌─(History)──────────────────────────────────────────


 ─(Enter your command, please) ─────────────┬─(Database)─
                                            │
├───────────────────────────────────────────┴───────────
│ Send with Return, PF1=Gold, PF2=Help, PF3=Leave, PF1 PF3=Quit
```

The cursor is set to the 'enter command' frame, and the user now types :

BASE CORR

which calls up the correspondence database by name.

The line at the bottom of the screen always contains a reminder[1] of the 'function keys' set up on the terminal to call standard system or 'help' functions. The 'database' box holds the name of the current database, and the 'history' box builds up a record of the steps in the search so far. All user commands (except 'help', 'leave' and 'quit') are typed into the command box.

---

[1] Warning! This is a much more supportive *command line* system than most users of the on-line bibliographic systems have learned to deal with!

TRIP puts the count of all of the records (99) at the top of the 'history'. Now search for correspondence about the university system :

FIND system AND universities   *(and the system replies)*

S=2 <2> F SYSTEM AND UNIVERSITIES   *(F short for FIND)*

so we have two records from the second search. But, of course, it could have been 'university', so maybe some records are being missed. Try :

FIND system AND universit#   *(using # to truncate)*

S=3 <18> F SYSTEM AND UNIVERSIT#

Now the screen looks like this :

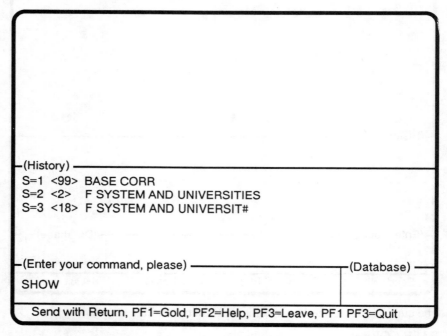

```
┌─(History) ─────────────────────────────────────────────
│ S=1 <99> BASE CORR
│ S=2 <2>  F SYSTEM AND UNIVERSITIES
│ S=3 <18> F SYSTEM AND UNIVERSIT#
│
│
├─(Enter your command, please) ──────────────────(Database) ──
│ SHOW                                          │
│                                               │
├───────────────────────────────────────────────
│ Send with Return, PF1=Gold, PF2=Help, PF3=Leave, PF1 PF3=Quit
```

To look at the records found in the last search the user then enters the SHOW command (which has lots of format options not illustrated here!) and the first record in the retrieved set will appear on the screen, temporarily over-writing the 'history' window. To see the following record, NEXT is used; or to scroll down the one on the screen at any time, MORE. A record on any other retrie-ved list can be seen by adding its serial number to the SHOW command, like SHOW S=2. The display, using a 'default' format set up by the system administrator as an easy-to-use option to suit most searches, then looks like the following screen :

```
┌─────────────────────────────────────────────────────────────┐
│                                                               │
│     Database CORR                    Mats G Lindquist         │
│                                      Paralog AB               │
│                                      Box 2284                 │
│                                      S-103 17 Stockholm       │
│     Dear Mats                        23rd December 1984       │
│                                                               │
│     Please could you let me know how the conversion from 3RIP to TRIP │
│     is going for large databases. There is some interest here in at least │
│     one such system, in a utility rather than a university installation. │
│                                                               │
│     The target hardware is a large DEC VAX, or possibly a pair of │
│     closely linked VAX cpus.  Language is English at present. │
│                                                               │
│     Yours sincerely                  Ashford Associates Ltd   │
│                                      72, Harrow Lane          │
│     John Ashford                     Maidenhead  SL6 7PA  UK  │
│  ─(Enter your command, please) ──────────────────(Database) ──│
│                                              │                │
│                                              │                │
│    Send with Return, PF1=Gold, PF2=Help, PF3=Leave, PF1 PF3=Quit │
└─────────────────────────────────────────────────────────────┘
```

(The example is realistic, but fictitious!) 'System' and 'university' have been found, and on some terminals would be highlighted.

PRINT would send the results of the designated search to a print queue.

Alternative forms of search command include :

- FIND price OR lease   (FIND uses all the index files)

- FIND price NOT lease

- FIND S=3 AND day>1985-06-01

  where the form S=3 combines the result of a previous search with the current command, and the day> *value* is a range test.

If the user is not sure of the content of the database vocabulary, a command of the form - DISPLAY *word#* will show a window of all words in the index beginning with those letters. Thus DISPLAY tex# might yield :

    T=1 <1> TEXAN   (DISPLAY uses only the word list file)
    T=2 <8> TEXT
    T=3 <5> TEXTS
    T=4 <3> TEXTUAL   (and so on)

STOP ends the session

3 Inside retrieval: how it works

This chapter looks in some detail at the structure and organisation of the text retrieval part of a total information management system. This is the *foundation* for the majority of text-only applications, and also for the recent developments in multi-format information processors dealing with graphics and other images.

The approach followed by almost all commercially viable systems[1] is to work with three main files - the **text** file containing information as originally input; a corresponding **inverse** file (or 'word list', or 'concordance') in which all the useful words from the text file are arranged in alphabetic order, and indexed; and a **pointer** file which leads to actual occurrences of words in the text. (Alternative methods will be described in chapters 10 - 13.) The parser in the input processor selects 'words', matches them with the existing inverse file, to identify those such as 'and', 'is', 'to' which make up much of normal text but have little retrieval value, and label them as **stop** words, so that they are not further indexed. A **word** is usually defined to be a string of alphanumeric characters (that is, A to Z and 0 to 9) bounded by spaces or 'special characters', but options may be set to include or exclude pure numbers, specials like hyphen and underline within text strings, and **go** words, where a word will be accepted for indexing only if it occurs on a preset control list (chapter 4).

When a new word is found in the text, it is added to the word list. For every word (other than a stop word), the count of its occurrences is updated, and a pointer added to a list for that word marking where it was found - addressing the sub-file or 'chapter' of the database, text record (or article), section, paragraph, and word position within the paragraph. Some systems recognise 'sentence' as a level. Figure 3.1 shows this structure, using only a few words from each text record for simplicity.

Retrieval functions

Some functions are based on the inverse file directly. A user is normally provided with a view of a section of the inverse file, so that similar words may be seen together. Truncation of terms for searching, so that plurals and other inflections are selected together, is directly handled by matching on the 'first n characters' - for example, PERMA* would match with 'PERMALLOY' and 'PERMANENT' but not with 'PERMEABLE' or 'PERMIAN'. In some

---

[1]   Referred to, usually, as 'inverted file' systems

Figure 3.1 : Text and inverse files

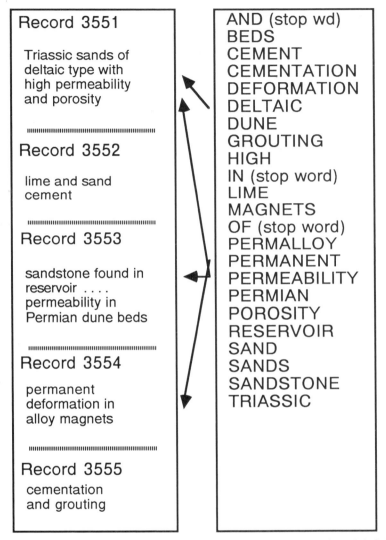

applications, typically chemical information systems, internal and left-hand truncation (sometimes called 'wild card' searching) is valuable for dealing with words like SUL?UR for which there are alternative spellings, and chemical names like ?CRESOL which could have prefixes *ortho-*, *para-*, and *meta-*. Synonyms, defined by the user or database administrator, are set as links between equivalent words in the inverse file. At a further level, a thesaurus of words and phrases arranged to reflect their meaning, may be constructed with the inverse file elements as its lowest level terms. This is similar to the traditional printed subject index, though it may be less formal in some practical cases, or detailed in others - especially bio-medical databases.

The way in which pointer lists may be represented is shown in figure 3.2. In the inverse file, it is necessary to make allowance for the variable length of natural words and typically an upper indexing limit of 30 characters is chosen. At the pointer list stage, all fields are of fixed length, and with this simple format processing can be optimised. Sections are coded internally, but the user would see the corresponding 'names' such as title, author, summary, data, action chosen to suit the information concerned. 'Sentence' is used as an indexing level in some systems. In others it bounds the 'co-location' or acceptable spacing of search terms to be taken together.

Figure 3.2 : Pointer list for words in Figure 3.1

Word	Frequ.	File	Document	Para.	Word#
PERMEABILITY	2	1	3551	2	8
		1	3553	5	7
PERMIAN	1	1	3553	5	9
SAND	1	1	3552	1	4
SANDS	2	1	3551	2	2
		1	3667	1	6
SANDSTONE	1	1	3553	5	2
TRIASSIC	1	1	3551	2	1

Inverse file --------------- Pointer list ---

The depth to which indexing is carried out varies between commercial products, and becomes noticeable especially in full text applications, where the ability to search on phrases and on words in close association using 'word level' indexes directly gives performance gains. Systems such as **BASIS** and **DOCUMASTER**, which gain in speed of simple retrievals by indexing only to whole document, or to paragraph level, must resort to slower sequential string searching for the final stages of phrase or related word searches.

Searches in the text database are made by interactive use of a Boolean query format[1]. A query of the form :

FIND WORD1 <u>operator</u> WORD2 ?

is processed as follows. FIND sets up the search mode. Each word in the query is looked up in the inverse file to check that it is not a stop word, and its frequency is stored. The pointer list for the word is then accessed to get the corresponding list of pointers.

---

[1] This approach works effectively in practice, but has a number of short-comings. For discussion and some alternatives, see chapter 10.

Figure 3.3 : 'Command language' form of dialogue

The following dialogue uses the **BASIS** system and searches in a database of press cuttings. The user input is shown, for clarity, in *italic*, the section headings in the cuttings documents in **BOLD CAPS**, and the general computer output in plain text. Comments are in parentheses.

Enter your request
1/ *find subject = aviation*
*   1   1/   **subject** = aviation   (1 cutting found, first search)
2/ *display headline, date, reporter*

Item 1
HEADLINE   Britain plans its space shuttle
PUB.DATE   06-FEB-86
REPORTER   Press Association

2/ *look subject = n**   (List subjects starting with the letter 'n')
        .ITEMS.   **TERMS**
A   1   **SUBJECT** = NATIONAL CRIMES
                   USE **SUBJECT** = CRIMES-NATIONAL   (Thesaurus in use)
B   2   **SUBJECT** = NAVY
C   18   **SUBJECT** = NUCLEAR ACCIDENTS
D   3   **SUBJECT** = NUCLEAR ARMS
        etc, to
J   3   **SUBJECT** = NUCLEAR WASTE
End of terms with your stem
Pick letters to combine
3/   *c-j*   (Selects all to do with NUCLEAR)
        41 items saved as set 2
Continue picks or requests
4/   *display subject, headline for 1-2*   (View part of first two items found)

Item 1
SUBJECT   NUCLEAR ACCIDENTS, WEATHER
HEADLINE   Britain keeps watch over nuclear plume

Item 2
SUBJECT   COUNCILLORS, NUCLEAR SURVIVAL
HEADLINE   Denial over fall-out query before council

5/ *find subject = pop and story= flower**   (* stems from the right)
*   3   3/   **SUBJECT** = pop   (3 found for 'pop')
*   2   4/   **STORY** = flower*   (2 found for flower*)
*   1   5/   **SUBJECT** = pop AND **STORY** = flower*   (1 has both)
6/   *display story*   (look at full text)

John Lydon - now with carrot-thatch dreadlocks - ranted his way through an evening of subversive heavy rock to satisfy his fans.

Nostalgia merchants were soon jumping up and down to Pretty Vacant, and old PIL favourites such as Flowers of Romance and Public Image were best received by the near sell-out crowd.

Johnny has finally come home and the man who provoked . . . . (etc)   (The **bold** print highlights the context of the selected word 'Flowers')

17

The 'operator' set normally comprises Boolean AND, OR and NOT. These are used to process the pointer lists, so that under AND only those pointers occurring in both lists, and under OR those occurring in either or both, are retained. The NOT operator acts to exclude designated terms. The final retrieved list indexes directly those text records which satisfy the terms of the query. So far all query processes have used the easily handled inverse file and pointer lists; only when the user asks for a display of the results of the search is access required to the more awkward text file in the original format.

When the query is simple, and the search scope is over whole text records :

> **FIND** TRIASSIC or PERMIAN ?

then only the file and record level pointers (1:3551, 1:3553 in the figure) are required. If, however, sections in a record (title, or geodata for example) are used to limit the scope of the search, or if phrases are used, then the pointers down to word level are applied. A query looking for 'permeability' within three words of 'Permian' would use this feature :

> **FIND** ((PERMEABILITY within 3 of
>
> PERMIAN) in geodata) or JONES in author ?

where 'in geodata' and 'in author' limit the search to paragraphs falling within those sections of the text record. Parentheses may be used freely for clarity, or to ensure that the Boolean relations are interpreted in the correct order. Figure 3.3 shows a 'real life' example.

Display functions

The display stage has several distinct steps. The first is to report the number of text records retrieved - 'none' leads to re-thinking the search, usually looking at the frequency of occurrence of the search terms by using the view facility. 'Too many', which in practice usually means more than twenty, but varies with the length of the records and the type of application, invites reduction of the retrieved list, by combining the current list of pointers with more search criteria. Given a retrieved list of moderate length, the user may choose to display a short version of each record, a selected set of sections of one or more records, or the full retrieved texts. The formats shown in figure 3.3 are fiarly typical of the basic functions provided in all packages.

In order to develop and enhance the basic functions, and to allow tailoring of particular applications to users' needs, macro processors have been added to some systems. In their simplest form these were no more than command files of standard query and display instructions which could be run as search profiles whenever a database was updated, to provide user defined subject searches. Later, they came to include more advanced formatting commands, access to internal variables such as time, date, number of records retrieved, simple arithmetic on numeric values and so on.

Figure 3.4 : An Online Public Access Catalogue (OPAC)

BRS/SEARCH and the MNS command language provide a 'panel' interface for the user. Adapted, with permission, from Prowse, S G, Use of BRS/SEARCH in OPAC experiments. Program, vol. 20, no. 2, April 1986. The subject area is 'education'.

The command stage is set out like this - user input in **bold** :

Command? **Select Title**	Use | <- | key to correct typing
Please type any words from the title	(Press ENTER key at end)
-> **Education**	

The search response is presented as follows :

SElect Title EDUCATION	Query 1	631 Titles retrieved

	TITLE	AUTHOR
1	The education of the black child in Britain the myth of multiracial education	Stone, M
2	Social studies in secondary education	Armstrong, D G
3	Children with special needs : a survey of special education	Lilly, M S

. . . . . etc . . . . .

Command? (Title number or from list below) and press ENTER key

FOrward (to see next page)	SElect (to restrict search)	UNdo selection
BAck (to see previous page)	INclude (to broaden search)	CLear
HElp	EXclude (to discard titles)	HIstory of search

Figure 3.4 shows an example taken from a study of online public access catalogues (OPAC) at the Centre for Catalogue Research, Bath. In this case, a set of high level command language routines was applied to protect the user from the difficulties perceived in reading records in the MARC[1] database, and make searching and display simple and easy for the user.

Another common application is command modification, where the names of macros replace the standard query and display commands for new and occasional users who do not need the whole range of facilities. An example is the public access World Reporter database (BRS/SEARCH), where on-line users need only learn the simple GET and PICK commands, to search for a word or phrase, and to refine their search respectively; thereafter HEADLINE, CONTEXT and TEXT show sensible sections of retrieved news items.

---

[1] MARC - for MAchine Readable Catalogue - is a widely used international exchange format for catalogue records (ISO 2709). Its internal complexities stem from its huge range of data elements and from its dual use as a typesetting source for major national bibliographies.

Other applications of macros include gateways to the operating system from minimal commands at the terminal - STATUS users on IBM MVS systems call the ISPF programmer aids and text editing services from inside the text retrieval processes. Some use operating system charge data to advise users of search costs. The gateway is particularly important as a way to handle optical disc storage of document images - which is of importance in large scale office automation. Macros have also been used for foreign language versions of English language-based software products.

Limitation of space usage

The use of inverse files and pointer lists tends to consume storage space on disc, typically at a rate of as much extra as the original text for the other files. Some systems (BRS/SEARCH assembler version for example) offer an option to compress the text itself, using standard sequential algorithms. This saves disc space at the expense of packing and unpacking complexity and processing when records are displayed. Alternatively, the use of a restricted 'pass' vocabulary can, in suitable cases and with suitable care over the subject matter, very much reduce the scale of the word list and pointer files without loss of retrieval effectiveness. CAIRS is particularly well adapted to this approach.

Several techniques have been applied to reduction of space taken up by both the word list and the pointer lists. They tend to be programmers' craft rather than formal methods, and the actual application varies widely from product to product. Those interested in the details may wish to refer to Choueka et. al. (1988) for 'prefix omission' and 'variable length storage of pointers'; any standard computer science text for 'binary trees' (B-Trees) to index word tokens; or Ashford and Scott (1978) for an early application of 'minimal incremental discriminants' in the ordering of variable length text items such as phrases and author-title entries. Much more is buried in the code of the better performing products and the private notebooks of their developers than has ever been published.

4 The parsing process

The process of scanning a text for a database, separating it into correct words or tokens[1] and placing references in the appropriate inverse and pointer files, is referred to as **parsing**. Although this is a fairly complex operation, it comprises only a small subset of the linguistic operations sometimes included under that description, and takes no account (at present, at least) of grammatical structures or semantic implications. Cercone and McCalla (1986) and King (1983) provide an accessible review of these wider issues, and of the potential links to work in artificial intelligence. Even in the narrower sense used here, three processes run together - fitting the text into the structure of the document; determining its constituent parts (words, or tokens); and matching these tokens with predetermined lists of words or phrases to mark their status in the information context of the database.

Text structures

The structural aspect is usually easiest. All text database systems provide some level of formatting of records, to allow the electronic form to match the practical layout and subdivisions of the 'outside' document (see chapter 2, for an example from TRIP). A typical set of structure options would include :

> **Free text** : This falls into a variable length field text containing unbounded, or at least long (> 10,000 characters), text, subdivided only into paragraphs and sentences. It is normally indexed as word tokens, where a token is a contiguous (up to 30 characters, say) string from an indexable set bounded by 'space' or a member of a 'non-indexable' set (+ - , * & # / ( ) etc) or an 'invisible text' mark (see **Text acquisition**). This may be augmented by the identification of 'phrases' from a list, or from markings in the text (see **Subject enrichment**).

> A *sentence end* is marked by either a paragraph end (below) or by the occurrence of combinations like[2] :

> text. CrUCtext   if CrCr is defined as the *paragraph end*
> text.ΔUCtext
> text!ΔUCtext   (as in : ". . . thisΔafternoon!ΔSoonΔthereΔwill . . .")

---

[1]   token : a word, or what, after re-definition, we choose to treat as a word.

[2]   Cr is used to mean 'carriage return and line feed'; Δ means 'space'; UC means 'upper case'.

One or two systems (INFO-DB+ in a future release, for example) will soon carry lists of exception cases, such as 'Inc. Ltd. lb. etc. mm. k.' etc. which require a following UC letter, so that allowance can be made for the problematic false endings like 'according to Name Inc.Δ27Δpeople . . .' - and its analogues.

A *paragraph end* is usually defined as CrCr, which includes ΔCrCr, CrCrΔ, and ΔCrCrΔ depending on the typist and the word processor. It *may* be defined as Cr alone (as in MacAuthor, which is being used to prepare this text), in which case .CrUCtext is a sentence *and* a paragraph division. Some systems allow a special marker ($$P in STATUS for example) to force recognition of a paragraph ending.

Problem cases do, in fact, occur in both sentence and paragraph endings, and occasionally result in false constructions. Consider :

---- gone!)?" Δ "Whoever ----"

---- morcilla!' Δ '¿QuéΔesΔeso?'

---- lugarite.)"'.Δ '33ΔScottishΔgeologists - - -'

none of which is too far-fetched, especially in full text applications.

Structured text : This usually takes the form of fixed length fields containing text strings. These may be indexed either as word tokens as in free text ($\leq$ 30 characters each); or as a single keyword[1] term or phrase (usually $\leq$ 60 characters each); or as a chain of keywords separated by a designated character, of which ';' is most common. In the last two forms, characters such as Δ which normally separate words are included in a single string[2] representing the text phrase, as in 'TEXTΔRETRIEVAL'.

There are some variants. Sometimes a phrase in a keyword field is analysed both as a phrase *and* as its constituent words. STATUS, where some implementations lack *field* facilities, has instead a 'marked text' concept, where *#name* is a marker followed by a special text segment which may be date, integer, real number, special characters or a phrase in parentheses (). (3 parsers out of four will, by the way, have trouble finding the beginning of this sentence!)[3]

Text acquisition

The processing of **input text** involves selection of a field into which text will be routed, and the copying of word tokens into a temporary store, together with field location pointers, as input to the indexing programs which update

---

[1] keyword : an inserted word or phrase of high retrieval value.

[2] string : that is, a piece of data with whose structure we are unconcerned.

[3] Every self-respecting book on language needs a self-referential twist somewhere.

the inverse file or word list and the related pointer files. A useful auxiliary facility, not always provided, is to list 'new words' - some of which commonly turn out to be spelling errors.

The boundaries of a token are normally :

- Beginning of a free text or structured text field
- Semi-colon ; or 'quote' marks in a keyword field (so not Δ)
- End of field
- Blank Δ (except in phrases in keyword fields)
- Characters used as wild cards in string searches (often * % and !)
- Characters used in truncation (* #) and for synonyms & thesaurus
- Parentheses () and quote ' used in formatting queries
- The 'invisible text' on and off character (commonly |)
- Cr and Lf   (carriage return and line feed)
- Other non alphanumeric characters unless designated as 'indexable' - the usual characters included under this option are _ + - / and : *because* the semicolon ; is commonly used as a phrase mark and the comma is unmanageable due to its frequency.

In a structured text keyword field, single quotes may be used to force a phrase to enclose blank characters. This is used in keyword and synonym handling. Case is optionally treated as 'all lower', or as 'all lower except for tokens consisting entirely of upper case characters' (eg IBM, NATO) where the difference is maintained. Diacritic marks and European characters such as é è ô ø å ∂ ç ß ¿ ¡ extend the working set in good implementations, but sometimes take two characters in internal format and are then difficult to retrieve and to show on screen.

A special case is the invisible text mark used in some systems to bound strings of mark-up characters derived from word processors or typesetters (BASIS, DM, BRS/SEARCH, STATUS on Wang computers, ORACLE*Text). This formatting text is stored in the main body, but is not indexed, nor is it normally displayed when the text is viewed.

Conflation, or stemming, is sometimes applied (more in research systems than in commercial products, and more in inflected languages like Finnish than in English) to reduce the many variants of a word to its single stem. This is more logical, but not necessarily more practical, than simple truncation (Lennon et al., 1981). The Paralog TRIP package provides an option to leave its parsing SCAN utility, and call an external routine to process the current word or phrase. A Finnish customer has attacked the quite difficult problem of stemming in that language using this facility, and other similar applications are envisaged.

Consideration must be given to the treatment of pure numbers. Current practice in free text processors is to offer an option to index digit strings or not, with 'keyed fields' used to handle 'real' formats. Given the availability of numeric processing in structured database systems with text (chapter 7), a stronger option is probably to offer a general choice to index 'real' or not, and then to treat '.' between strings of pure digits as indexable.

A phrase like "Let e be 2.718." would then yield one of :

let	let	let	let	let
e	e	be[1]	2[2]	0.2718E1[3]
be	be	2.718	718	
2.718[4]	2[5]			
	718			

In all practical text indexing systems, each word is matched against a list of 'stop' words to determine if it is to be excluded from further processing - usually because it occurs so frequently as to be of little value in retrieval. In some instances this step reduces the volume of the word list and the pointer files by as much as 45% of the raw value.

Subject enrichment

This is used here to mean :

- The addition to an existing text of keyword and phrases either freely, or from a thesaurus or other controlled vocabulary;

- Marking existing words or phrases in the text as 'indexable strings', so that, for example, **proper names** remain as coherent units;

- 'Binding' so that compound names such as 'A Sand' (in the Brent Oil and Gas Field) do not lose the 'A' as a stop word - a typical tie is a concordable underscore, thus A_Sand, indexed as a_sand;

- Passing of words or phrases (however marked) against a 'pass' or 'go' list to ensure that *only* acceptable terms are indexed;

- Recognition that a term belongs to a synonym group, and replacement, if necessary, by a designated preferred term;

- Identification of phrases in the text on a pre-determined list, and then indexing both as individual words and as complete phrases - so that 'North Sea' would lead to 'north', 'sea', and 'northΔsea' for the index. This avoids slow searches where the components are both frequent in the text, but the phrase is relatively uncommon.

---

[1]   *e* was lost, being in italic

[2]   . . . and 'be' was chosen as a stop word

[3]   Floating point format for 'real' number

[4]   Fixed point format for 'real' number

[5]   Point . is here not concordable and so forms two words - '2' and '718'

Since the wordlist is in alphabetic order of terms and keyword or synonym bound phrases, it is easy and useful to offer a window of terms adjacent to a selected term to aid vocabulary choice. A more sophisticated approach to-subject enrichment involves the use of a thesaurus which operates, in effect, by setting up ties between items in the wordlist which are not in simple alphabetical order, to maintain semantic rather than syntactic relations.

The standard thesaurus ties are :

Term1 BT Term2	Broader term
Term1 NT Term2	Narrower term(s)
Term1 USE Term	Term2 is preferred
Term1 UF Term2	Term1 is preferred (use for)
Term1 see Term2	Reference for indexer
Tem1 RT Term2	Related term
Term1 scope note	Explanatory text

For example, and simplifying somewhat :

Lava BT volcanic rocks	Tholeiite SEE dolerite
Lava NT andesite	Ring complex RT central complex
Lava NT basalt	Ring complex NT Ardnamurchan
Basalt BT lava	Volcanic : *scope note* - used here
Trap USE dolerite	for extrusive, and *high level*
Dolerite UF trap	intrusive rocks.

BT, NT, USE/UF and RT are reflexive pairs. Terms are often phrases. There is theoretical argument as to whether a term can have more than one broader term. For more on thesauri see Aitchison and Gilchrist (1987).

Those packages most strongly directed towards the *special library* user - ASSASSIN, CAIRS, MORPHS for example - tend to have the widest repertoire of subject and indexing control features. TINMAN can be so rich in relational ties between fields that the user has the feeling of browsing more in the subject concepts than in the text of the documents - and in the field of the natural sciences in particular, this appears to be well liked and effective.

Frequency distribution of vocabulary

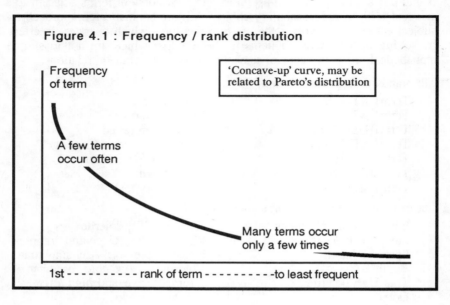

Figure 4.1 : Frequency / rank distribution

Frequency of term

'Concave-up' curve, may be related to Pareto's distribution

A few terms occur often

Many terms occur only a few times

1st - - - - - - - - - - rank of term - - - - - - - - - -to least frequent

For many text databases, a plot of the frequency of individual terms against their ranked order of frequency yields a curve like figure 4.1. The skewed distribution of frequencies[1] can cause problems in storing the pointer lists efficiently. In the upper left part of the curve are found the relatively few very frequent terms parsed from the database. Typically there is a mixture of simple articles and conjunctions, and commonly used substantive words. Among the articles and conjunctions are found *and, is, are, was, were, for, to, by, it, them, a, an, which* and so on. Some care is needed in setting up stop lists, as, for example, in a database on information technology the incorporation of *is, us* and *it,* alias *IS, US* and *IT,* can seriously reduce the number of access points in the subject matter. Similarly *as* = arsenic, *be* = beryllium and *in* = indium are not helpful as stop words in metallurgical references.

The best practice is probably to set no stop words at all at first, and to inspect the vocabulary as text is added before removing only those which are evidently high frequency, and have been subjected to an imaginative search for cryptic homographs. In most systems to make a word a stop word is easy and cheap; the reverse involves at least partial, and sometimes complete re-parsing and re-indexing.

---

[1] Pareto's distribution : Such 'concave upwards' distributions of frequency against rank are similar to those investigated by the Italian economist Vilfredo Pareto (1848-1923) in his work on the distribution of property and incomes in capitalist societies. In theory, the logarithm of the frequency is directly related to the rank of the term. Similar distributions have been noted in many other fields.

The other high frequency terms are useful, relevant words in the subject. They would be *steel* and *concrete* in a civil engineering database; *case* and *judgement* in legal material. Frequencies of 30,000 to 75,000 are not uncommon for the top four or five useful words in a 200 megabyte text file, and the shape of the curve appears to remain similar as database size increases.

In the lower right part of the curve are found many words with frequencies of one only. These include highly specific terms, of limited utility except for 'known item' retrieval such as a book by a clearly remembered author; and also the detritus of spelling errors, unrecognised synonyms, failures in the parser and the like. Periodic cleaning out of the errors is desirable to improve storage efficiency and both precision and recall in retrieval.

The really useful zone lies in the middle of the curve, where most terms fall between 20 and 2,000 postings. Here the retrieval times are good - close to the design optimum for the software - and the effectiveness of the search in information terms is also most satisfactory. In a total vocabulary of 100,000 words (excluding stop words) it is not unusual to find that the useful zone comprises less than 15% of the total vocabulary.

If the curve is re-plotted with the logarithm of the frequency against rank of the term, the result is often, in practice, not a single straight line which is intuitively expected, but a series of segments roughly corresponding to the three zones discussed above (Figure 4.2). The reasons for this are not too clear, and in any case formal and quantitative treatment of this type of distribution - as opposed to its qualitative, explanatory value - is somewhat intractable (Brookes, 1984).

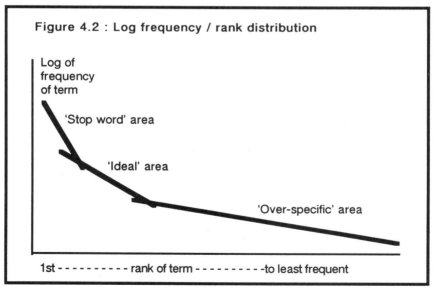

Figure 4.2 : Log frequency / rank distribution

Log of frequency of term

'Stop word' area

'Ideal' area

'Over-specific' area

1st - - - - - - - - - rank of term - - - - - - - - -to least frequent

5 Applications: mostly text

In this chapter, applications are discussed more or less as they developed historically, from **full text** (FTX) applications, where the whole of a text or text compatible source is held on-line, through the **indicative text** (ITX) method which for a decade overtook full text in the number of working systems, and leads into a wide variety of multi-media information systems. Re-

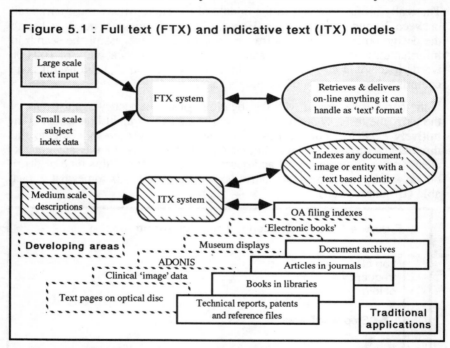

Figure 5.1 : Full text (FTX) and indicative text (ITX) models

cently, full text applications have become more frequent, and in late 1988 there is a balance between the two approaches (Figure 5.1).

Full text applications

The essence of a full text system is that the user, as the result of a successful search, has the 'facts' or 'answers' directly on the screen, from a single source. The limitation is that the information must either be in text (ASCII or EBCDIC) format, or in a form which the database handler can select and de liver to an appropriate terminal, and in an intrinsically text-directed context. Typical text-only projects using full text information are transcripts of news items; legal statutes and cases; standards and safety regulations; records of hazardous chemicals and their emergency treatment; research programmes and reports; product directories; software and equipment fault reports and diagnoses; catalogues of engineering components and supplies.

There is often an initial problem to be solved in the acquisition of the text in computer-readable form. A DIN A4 (or quarto) page of typescript yields 2,500 to 4,000 characters of input - much less than the corresponding 50,000 bytes if it were scanned as a raster image, but costly to re-key if it cannot be acquired from word processor files, or by optical character recognition (OCR). An efficient, motivated keyboard operator in a typing pool typically delivers between ten and twelve million characters of read and corrected text per year. OCR units have become cheaper and more effective, but the scanned text still normally requires proof reading and editing if the exact content is critical - as it usually is with full text retrieval! Given reasonably clean input, in a standard fount and one or two sizes, conversion at 30 characters per second is achievable on a unit based on a micro computer and costing less than £20,000. This delivers 100 million characters or more of converted text per year, allowing for checking, so that on a large job the economics are much better than re-keying. Newsprint, unfortunately, appears to be unsatisfactory as a source for OCR, and direct transcription of newspaper typesetting tapes loses last minute, often urgent, removals of portions of 'rejected' text from the made up pages. Voice to text conversion will have many applications in office automation, but is still in the research stage.

If the text is written in formal, professional language, it may contain a predictable and specific vocabulary which enables all retrievals to be performed by searching in the body of the document as entered. Auxiliary input is then restricted to title, date of issue, author, security status and similar small additions. Such cases are often found in company contracts databases; personnel records; research and marketing data; and fault reporting systems. The style may, on the other hand, be largely informal (much administrative paper), or may deal with subject areas such as education, geology, medicine or physics, where vocabularies are either very complex or rapidly evolving, and it is necessary for efficient searching to add **subject terms** or **keywords** chosen from a **thesaurus**. This is sometimes referred to as '**subject enrichment**'. A thesaurus of such terms may act either as an interactive classification guide, or as an aid to the user in retrieval from the database.

Searching generally follows the pattern described in chapter 3, using Boolean combinations of words or their truncated stems. In the display stage, as the full text record normally extends over several screens, special commands are used. These are commonly a **context** command, to show the text adjacent to a chosen term in the text record, and **zoom** to allow similar quick access in units of pages. **Browsing**, either within a long text, or, if the natural sequence of the records on the database is systematic, between 'adjacent' items, is appreciated by users in the exploratory stages of research studies. A **routing** option, to send selected text to a system file to be typeset or, for numeric data, to be plotted, is also found to be of value. A typical syntax (STATUS on IBM, command verbs in **bold**) might look like :

Q french @ language ?	(User input)
7 articles satisfy this question	(System replies)
Display File='work.data' (NAME,LOCN) ALL	(Write to file)
Tweak work.data	(A user macro)

A practical difficulty found with full text systems is that of the time and resources taken up in updating following additions of new material. Since a modest application is likely to have 50 Mb of text on-line, plus a further 50-75 Mb of indexes and auxiliary files, and may add new data at 25% per year or more, the problem is not unexpected, but it does make frequent amendments and small additions fairly costly in computer resources. The two-to-one overhead for indexing arises from the storage required firstly for the concordance, one record for each new word which is not a stop word; and secondly from the pointer lists, with one record for each occurrence. As the database grows, the overhead ratio slowly falls.

Update strategy

A few packages - BRS/SEARCH 'C' version and STATUS; and DM, INFOText and INFO-DB+ among the R.DBMS systems (see chapter 7) - allow immediate, on-line updating of new records entered at the terminal. Although this adds to the internal complexity of multi-user software it finds applications in 'accident and incident' systems used by police and other organisations to build up files of current reports as they become available - where the immediacy justifies the extra running costs. More commonly, a batch update process is used following one of two strategies. Systems such as BRS/SEARCH (IBM assembler[1] version) and IBM STAIRS form a separate database for each tranche of new material, and then permit searching across all databases in the same 'family'. When the consequent run-time costs become noticeable, the databases are merged in a separate process into a single new set of files, and the cycle restarts. Others, (for example BASIS, BRS/SEARCH 'C' version, INFOText, STATUS) update a single database incrementally.

The effect is shown diagrammatically in Figure 5.2. Experience indicates that with few but large additions of new text, the 'separate files & merge' strategy usually comes out best. With small and frequent additions, the incremental approach gives lowest total costs. It is not unusual to find that a very efficient program - say the most fully optimised batch update utility of a ma-

---

[1] assembler : the lowest level of programming language in general use; it offers concise, fast running code at the expense of slower development, more difficult maintenance, and the need for specialist programmers.

ture product - uses less than one twentieth of the central processor and disc access resources taken up per record inserted or deleted, compared with on-line updating with the same product in a multi-user system. Since the cost of deleting a record is generally larger than that of insertion - more accesses to the index files are involved - some applications add new records interactively, but delete unwanted material in batch.

Figure 5.2 : Alternative update strategies

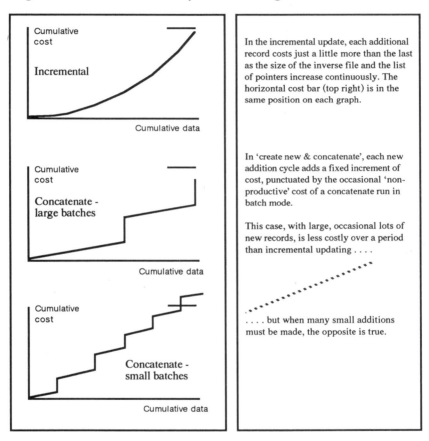

In the incremental update, each additional record costs just a little more than the last as the size of the inverse file and the list of pointers increase continuously. The horizontal cost bar (top right) is in the same position on each graph.

In 'create new & concatenate', each new addition cycle adds a fixed increment of cost, punctuated by the occasional 'non-productive' cost of a concatenate run in batch mode.

This case, with large, occasional lots of new records, is less costly over a period than incremental updating . . . .

. . . . but when many small additions must be made, the opposite is true.

Indicative text systems

The classic use of ITX has been the **bibliography,** of what one might *want* to look up in books or journals locally or elsewhere, or the **catalogue** of what *actually is held* in a library. The text record may be brief - author; title; date; classmark; abstract - or as full as a national bibliography entry. It depends on the size of the library, the complexity of the holdings, and whether records must be exchanged internationally with other centres - which usually leads to a requirement for MARC compatibility.

The cataloguing approach can easily be extended to records on microfilm; press cuttings; conventional filing systems; archives; and museum collections. The typical path is shown in the upper part of Figure 5.3. The 'module' which interprets the 'pointer' may well be a person noting down the reference, and indeed, there is some evidence that while bibliographic and cataloguing systems remain largely the province of the librarian, full text applications in general, and those specific ITX sources *which deliver results on-line*, are dominated by end users working directly with the system (Fries and Brown, 1988; Gurnsey and White, 1988a).

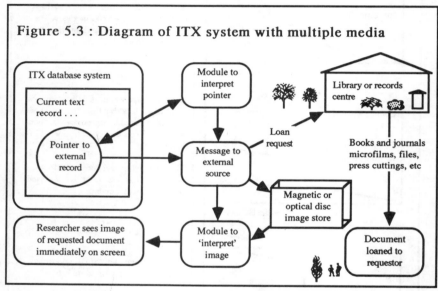

Figure 5.3 : Diagram of ITX system with multiple media

Although many libraries handling scientific, technical and medical information now depend heavily on ITX systems, they have not so far wholly satisfied their users over the delay in producing the document - from minutes to days - due to relying on stocks of paper records, or dealt satisfactorily with books already out on loan. The British Library ADONIS project is a current venture into regional delivery of page images from a source on compact discs (CD-ROM : chapter 9) and, if successful, may ease the document supply problems. So far it specialises in the bio-medical research field.

If records are held in electronic form - and this applies to non-indexed ASCII text; vector graphic data; bit maps of text and line diagram pages; fine raster images of half-tone 'pictures' - the desired information can be delivered quickly to the on-line user, and several enquirers may see the same record at once. This is a major gain, but introduces some complexity.

Apart from some special aspects of handling raster images from optical disc, which will be dealt with in more detail in chapter 9, a system must :

- Maintain and be able to identify 'pointers' to external files within the text records - and programs which scan text are less flexible than human readers, so sometimes there is the need for the user to 'point to' the external record identifier;

- Interpret the pointers when a user calls for a record, and generate a suitable message and system call to the external source;

- Retrieve the desired record and make it available to the ITX system, including dealing with 'not found', or 'no communications available', or 'Sorry, a system error occurred ID = 2', or the many other passing hazards of multiple applications;

- Interpret the external record, and present it to the user in a rational format, taking account of the terminal in use. (Figure 5.3)

Just how the linkages are achieved is very much operating system-dependent, and is also affected by the handlers for vector graphics or image file stores. The majority of working systems are one-off solutions, without, as yet, any standard harness products. They have also tended, in many commercial optical disc products, to adopt very basic indexing approaches, with a limited range of keys stored in fixed field files or relational databases.

An application has been reported at Jaguar Cars Limited, where illustrations (mostly line drawings) have been interpolated in the text of engineering quality standards; this uses STATUS and IBM's PMRS graphics handler in a VM/CMS environment. This project has a very strong direction towards 'showing the engineer all the necessary information' as an on-line, single service. In a quite different context, the BRS Colleague system collates the full text of clinical data sheets with images held on optical disc and presented on a second (video) terminal. The video image provides the necessary high resolution for the tissue photographs required by the professional users.

Figure 5.4 illustrates yet another engineering application, by London Regional Transport, where microfilm is the image medium, and 5.5 shows a full text application where, for legal information, text is the sole requirement.

As office digital image applications using optical discs move from high volume, simply-accessed office paper (insurance claims, for example, which are more or less self-indexing by client and date) to project management records or classified telephone directories - both currently being explored - the need for text-based access and retrieval is likely to make itself as prominent as it has been in the past with magnetic disc text storage.

Figure 5.4 : London Regional Transport drawings system

An application example of ITX plus microfilm at London Regional Transport - adapted, by permission, from an article in BRS Europe..UPDATE, Issue no. 1, Autumn 1987.

London Regional Transport (LRT) provides a road and railway public transport system covering the whole of the Greater London area. LRT consists (mainly) of the two limited companies :

- London Buses Ltd - the largest bus operator in Europe, with its fleet of 5,000 buses, and

- London Underground Ltd - with nine lines and 273 railway stations.

In order for London Underground engineering departments to deal with both everyday maintenance and major incidents, they maintain, in the Central Information Services Unit, a collection of more than half a million drawings of lines, stations and equipment - some dating back to the early 19th century. Prior to 1986, finding particular drawings or related correspondence involved searching in 400,000 index cards. Cross-references were required, especially when drawings were common to several sites. Finding drawings in this way was labour intensive and relied heavily on the skill and knowledge of staff.

In 1986, the indexing system was put on to BRS/SEARCH, using an IBM mainframe, and the corresponding drawings and documentation were microfilmed and stored on Kodak Intelligent Microfilm equipment. New documents are routed to a central location, and both filmed, and indexed on the text database using BRS/CABS, a form like page editor.

Engineers who require access to drawings or other papers can now access the BRS/SEARCH database from remote sites connected to the IBM network. When the document has been identified, a message is routed to the *Intelligent Microfilm* unit, and the record is printed for despatch to the user.

The system now provides a faster and more reliable service, with flexible cross referencing, and avoids the tedious and labour intensive tasks of index card filing, and searching in a large card catalogue.

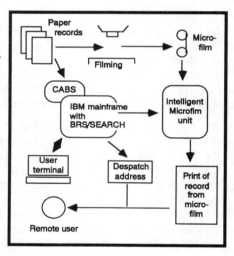

The use of microfilm with an automated search process is interesting. Other similar systems use 35mm aperture cards, but allow an operator to make the actual selection.

Figure 5.5 : Example of full text retrieval using STATUS

a) **Setting up a search for Times Law Reports** 'dated between 1st
January 1977 and 31st December 1988', where the **party** is
'Hillingdon Borough Council' and the **subject** is 'homeless and
abroad'. The 'number of reports retrieved' is inserted by the search
program after the user keys 'return'.

```
┌─────────────────────────────────────────────────────────────────────┐
│               STATUS INFORMATION MANAGEMENT SYSTEM                    │
│                     TIMES   LAW   REPORTS                             │
│                                                                       │
│  ─────────────────────────────────────────────────────────────────  │
│                                                                       │
│  Parties          Hillingdon London Borough Council                   │
│  Court            :                                                   │
│  Judge            :                                                   │
│  Dates                After   DAY 01 MONTH 01 YEAR 1977               │
│                   and Before  DAY 01 MONTH 01 YEAR 1988               │
│                                                                       │
│                                      AND                              │
│  Heading          :                                                   │
│  Abstract         Homeless  Abroad                                    │
│  Council          :                                                   │
│  Judgement        :                                                   │
│  Citation         :                                                   │
│  Ruling           :                                                   │
│  Argument         :                                                   │
│  Facts            :                                                   │
│  Opinion          :                                                   │
│  Full Report      :                                                   │
│                                                                       │
│  Number of reports retrieved = 52                                     │
│                                                                       │
│           Fill in the panel, then press Return to start the search    │
│                                                                       │
│  ─────────────────────────────────────────────────────────────────  │
│                                                                       │
│  Options: 1 Help  2 Info  3 Titles  5 Full Text  6 Context  7 STATUS commands 0 Quit│
└─────────────────────────────────────────────────────────────────────┘
```

This format is set up to operate solely in Boolean AND logic, but it is not
difficult to introduce OR and NOT conditions by the use of extra fields in the
display. All search fields may be edited, on screen, in page mode fashion.

The 'command line' is placed in a consistent position at the base of the
screen, so that the user always knows where to look for prompts[1]. Sometimes
it is practical to keep the same actual commands from screen to screen, but
when, as in this case the following display requires quite different actions, all
that can be done is to keep common prompts in the same place.

---

[1] That is, users of IBM PCs, their MS-DOS analogues, and many minicomputer
terminals will look there. The Macintosh style of commands, prompts and windows
placed at the top of the screen is found, by many, to be more comfortable, and as
'windows' spread to the MS-DOS environment, the preferred style may change.

Figure 5.5 : (continued)

b) The resulting output is laid out in a similar format :

```
Item *1 of 52                 TIMES LAW REPORTS              Row 1 of 105
═══════════════════════════════════════════════════════════════════════
```

Parties	Regina vs Hillingdon Borough Council
Court	Court of Appeal
Dates	£date 10:07:1980 *(Keyed field; chapter 4)*
Judges	Before Lord Denning, Master of Rolls, Lord Justice Waller
	and Lord Justice Dunn
Heading	Duty to homeless without local connection
Abstract	The duties imposed on housing authorities by the Housing (Homeless
	Persons) Act 1977, were held by the Court of Appeal to be owed to all
	homeless persons lawfully in this country, including those who came
	from abroad and had no local connection with any area of
	Great Britain.
	The Court dismissed an appeal by Hillingdon London Borough Council
	against an order of certiorari granted by the Divisional Court (The
	Times, February 28) to quash a decision by the Council that they owed
	no duty . . . . . .

Options : 1 Help 2 Prev 3 Next 4 Top 5 Bottom 6 Left 7 Right 8 Up 9 Down 0 Quit

(The Quit option returns to the Search panel)

6 Text retrieval in the office

In chapter 2 the reader was given a brief sample of what it is like to use one of the more approachable command language interfaces, using Paralog AB's TRIP as an example, and a demonstration database of correspondence documents. Now the same database, with the same structure, is presented as it would appear with the same TRIP software running under All-in-1, the DEC VAX office automation environment.[1]

From a general 'what is available' display, the user selects the search form by typing :   **SFO<return>**

A prompt for the name of the database invites the reply :   **CORR<return>** and the initial screen appears (Figure 6.1). If the user had not known the

Figure 6.1 : TRIP with All-in-1 - the initial display

```
┌─────── Searches in : CORR ─────────────────────────┐
│                                                     │
│                                                     │
│                                                     │
│                                                     │
│ ─────── Find Order ─────────────────────────────── │
│                                                     │
│                                                     │
└─────────────────────────────────────────────────────┘
                       Search Form
                 Include Search Sets : _____
   Content :    _____
   Author :     _____
   Title :      _____
   Created    from date : _____    to date : _____
   Keywords   _____
```

---

[1]   Strictly speaking, it is TDBS - the TRIP kernel - integrated with All-in-1

37

name of the database, then an entry of **<GOLD> <L>** would list the available databases. **<GOLD>** is a special command prefix key used in All-in-1 to provide a short cut to frequently used functions.

The search display is adapted to the database in use, and in this mode, the user asks 'questions' by filling in the lower part of the display as if it were a normal enquiry form. Suppose the query was for documents about a *system* The word 'system' is entered in the Content space, using the cursor controls on the keyboard[1] to move around if necessary, and <return> to search.

The screen records :

- **Search 1: 64 documents. CONTENT=system**

This is rather a lot, and can usefully be reduced to those written by Mats or Rolf.[2] Content still contains 'system', so 'Mats or Rolf' can be added to the query in the Author field. The result is shown on the screen in figure 6.2, where a date restriction has been made also. The Find Order box always contains the equivalent command form of the search order generated in

Figure 6.2 : TRIP with All-in-1 - the search form

```
┌─────────── Searches in : CORR ──────────────────────┐
│ - Search 1 : 64 documents.  CONTENT=system           │
│ - Search 2 : 27 documents.  CONTENT=system AND AUTHOR=(Mats │
│                             OR Rolf)                  │
│ - Search 3 : 25 documents.  CONTENT=system AND AUTHOR=(Mats │
│                             OR Rolf) AND CREATED>1983-01-01 │
│                             AND CREATED<1985-06-30    │
│ ──────────── Find Order ──────────────               │
│  FIND CONTENT=system AND AUTHOR=(Mats OR Rolf) AND    │
│  CREATED>1983-01-01 AND CREATED<1985-06-30            │
└──────────────────────────────────────────────────────┘

                        Search Form

                    Include Search Sets : _____

  Content :    system _____

  Author :     Mats or Rolf _____

  Title :      _____

  Created      from date : __830101__   to date : __850630__

  Keywords     _____
```

---

[1] ↑ → ← ↓ and ↰ (return)

[2] Real people!

TRIP, so that the way in which the contents of the form part have been interpreted can be verified, or, for a more specific query, edited. This sort of form-filling approach is sometimes called QBE - query by example.

Before considering how the results are displayed, suppose the search term had not been 'system' but a vaguer 'price' or 'pricing' or 'prix' (this is a multi-lingual database)? The entry 'pri' in Content followed by <GOLD> <L> finds the list of terms shown in figure 6.3, where PRI$ is treated as a truncated form.

Figure 6.3 : TRIP with All-in-1 - the list display

```
                          List of Terms

   Term:      CONTENT=PRI$
                                                  ┌──────────────┐
   Select:                                        │ 11 Terms found │
                                                  └──────────────┘

     1      (16)       PRICE
     2      (1)        PRICED
     3      (1)        PRICELIST
     4      (5)        PRICES
     5      (1)        PRIMARILY
     6      (3)        PRINCIPLE
     7      (5)        PRINCIPLES
     8      (2)        PRINTED
     9      (3)        PRIS
    10      (2)        PRISET
    11      (2)        PRIVATE
```

One, or several of these terms can be selected by cursor, and included in the next search as OR related terms.

Let's go back to display of the results of the figure 6.2 search. A summary listing of the retrieved documents is called up by <GOLD> <O>, figure 6.4. The layout of this display is a function of the database, and has been designed by the database administrator to suit the users.

Figure 6.4 : TRIP with All-in-1 - list of documents

```
                        List of found documents

 Title                  Author              Created     Modified

 3RIP Prices            Mats Lofstrom       1981-11-20  1981-11-20
 Telex from Sparkler Inst.  Mr Ron Smith    1984-06-13  1984-06-13
 Price request          Mr Adam Young       1981-11-09  1981-11-09
 3RIP Training Information  Orjan Leringe    1984-08-22  1984-08-22
 Price Information      Orjan Leringe       1984-07-11  1985-01-05
 Request for 3RIP Info. Laura Horney        1984-06-27  1986-06-27
 Send manuals           Peter Pannenbein    1984-06-06  1984-06-06
 Answer to John Ashford Jan Hultgren        1985-01-25  1985-01-25
 Licence fee            Mats G Lindquist    1984-01-24  1984-01-24
 Licence agreement      Orjan Leringe       1985-02-07  1985-04-01
 Letter from Mr Cook    Ted Cook            1983-12-01  1983-12-01
 Letter to Mr Smith     Mats G Lindquist    1983-12-02  1983-12-02
 New 3RIP version       Jan Svendsen        1983-10-30  1984-11-15
 Letter to Dr Willett   Orjan Leringe       1984-08-14  1984-08-14
```

The further options at this point include :

copy documents to a new folder within All-in-1

delete documents (if the user has this right)

browse the retrieved documents.

To browse in the retrieved set of documents, the command is <GOLD> <B>, and it displays a screen like figure 6.5. The upper part of the display shows the number of the search (as in figure 6.2, top panel), the All-in-1 data about where it is stored and its brief profile.

The user may scroll the current document in the window, step to the next, step back or leave the screen by using appropriate <GOLD> keys. In particular, <GOLD> <A> gives access to a group of All-in-1 file and folder management commands.

Figure 6.5 : TRIP with All-in-1 - browse screen

```
                              Browse
        Search Number:  5

        Folder:      Outgoing letters            Receiver:
        Title:       Answer to John Ashford
        Author:      Jan Hultgren

        Keywords:
        Created:     1985-01-25                  Modified: 1985-01-25

        or at least consider making some of these changes in the next release.

        TRIP adopts a very different basic structure from 3RIP, while retaining
        many of the earlier features which I hope you have come to appreciate.
        It has also being implemented for the DEC VAX machine, which will give
        us both widely available equipment and, we expect, good retrieval
        performance.

        Maybe we should arrange to meet with your client when next  you are in
```

In fairness to Paralog, from whose training manuals these examples and those of chapter 2 have been adapted, it should be made clear that only a small subset of the whole range of commands and options has been illustrated here. The intention has been to give a flavour of on-line, in both command mode (chapter 2) and page mode under an office automation system, using the same information in the same database structure. It was not meant to be a condensation of the system reference manuals!

TRIP and TDBS are not, of course, the only systems to have a working All-in-1 interface! An alternative, flexible, and particularly user-supportive version has recently been demonstrated in ASSASSIN, and by the end of 1988, most of the major system vendors should have operational interfaces.

7 Text content and data structures

In previous chapters attention has been directed to systems in which text is predominant. There are, however, many applications which contain too much text to fit readily into conventional DBMS structures, but in which the numeric data content - and the requirement to manipulate data - is also important. Other considerations which lead to a database choice include the need for reliable and efficient recovery from hardware failure, and clean roll-back of current transactions, and dealing with large populations of users over telecommunications networks. In some cases it is simply that an organisation has many numeric database applications, and a few text projects, and wishes to

---

Figure 7.1 :Search for data within text

Q #AGE < 35 + #SAL > 25000?   *(query)*
25 articles satisfy this question   *(reply)*

SubQ finance @ DEPARTMENT ? *(refine query)*
3 articles satisfy this question   *(reply)*

SORT #AGE D
VALUE (#SAL #AGE) ALL   *(list results)*
    31125   32
    24500   29
    39000   22
VALUE (#SAL #AGE) ALL File = 'name'

(Send the table to a 'system' file for processing)

(Example taken from 'command line' style within
  STATUS; here # is the special numeric prefix; and
  + means Boolean AND)

---

minimise the range of software packages to which users must accommodate themselves.

Most inverse file based retrieval systems, which were designed to handle mainly text, deal with data values in two ways. They may allow a section of a record to be declared as 'data' of some sort, (BASIS, BRS/SEARCH for example) or may provide for data in the text itself, identified by a reserved character prefix (#) as illustrated in Figure 7.1 (STATUS).

Figure 7.2 : Data and text structures in R.DBMS

Catalogue table

ISBN	Author	Title	Date
0-201-14502-2	Deitel, H M	An introduction to operating systems (Ed 1)	1984
0-201-19215-2	Date, C J	An introduction to database systems (Ed 4)	1986
0-86238-091-X	Oxborrow, E A	Databases and database systems	1986
0-442-31770-0	Burton, P F, Petrie, J H	The librarian's guide to microcomputers	1986

Locations table

ISBN	Copy no	Location	Issue status
0-201-14502-2	1	Z276	Short loan
0-201-14502-2	2	D:Z27	Standard
0-201-19215-2	1	Z225.9	Short loan
0-201-19215-2	2	Z225.9	Standard
0-201-19215-2	3	Z225.9	Standard
0-86238-091-X	1	R51	Reference
0-86238-091-X	2	Z225.9	Standard
0-442-31770-0	1	Z678.9	Short loan

Data definitions

ISBN is a character field, and also a key for both tables (relations)

Author is fixed length text
Title might be fixed or variable
Date is a number field
Copy number is a number field
Location is a character field
Issue status is a character field

(If a long abstract was needed, in a variable field, then Title would normally be kept down to 240 characters in a fixed field.)

In either case the data may be declared as integer, real, string, date and so on, and may be manipulated by simple arithmetic, range tests, sorting on value, and (for strings) wild card[1] searching. This works well when the data content of the record is a minor part, and the retrievals do not become too ambitious in numeric processing. Typical applications are :

• Search for documents written after a given date, or between dates, as shown in Figure 5.5;

• Inspect the CVs of all employees earning more than a certain annual salary, or with more than a number of years' service;

• List outstanding reported software faults, ordered by priority and date of entry.

If numeric and coded data form the main part of the record, or if logical and arithmetic manipulation are more important than search and retrieval, then an alternative approach through the use of a structured database management system with text extensions may be the best solution. Although there are a few examples where hierarchic or network DBMS packages have been successfully extended to deal with free text fields - ADABAS TRS from Software AG; INQUIRE from Infodata Systems Inc. in particular - they are large scale, mainframe, and relatively costly as text systems unless the package is already in use for conventional data processing. Many more products now use the relational database model as the starting point and this trend looks set to continue. The following account of relational databases is limited to the aspects necessary to deal with its text developments; those who wish a more thorough treatment of the underlying theory and data design principles for the *structured* part should consult Date (1986) or Oxborrow (1986).

In a relational database management system (R.DBMS for short) information is held in the form of tables (strictly relations) formed by selections of data values. The columns of these tables (domains) correspond to fields in conventional records, and each row (tuple) is an actual instance of the data, like a record in COBOL. It is generally desirable for data elements to be normalised to avoid problems with repeating groups and indexing consistency. This involves examining the structure and use of the data to form simple, coherent keys, and, as shown for ISBN in Figure 7.2, to form separate tables of the independent relations to which key values may refer. A high level query language, which may either be used for on-line enquiries, or embedded in other programs, makes it easy to build new tables, select data, sort results tables, and write reports. SQL[2] appears to be an acceptable, if sometimes theoretically disputable, *de facto* standard for R.DBMS interactions, though several sound and established systems have their own alternatives.

---

[1] wild card : a character such as * or # used to mean 'any one' or 'any contiguous set of' unknown characters within a word or phrase - provenance probably the gaming table.

[2] SQL : structured query language - often pronounced 'sequel'

Adding text to relational structures

When text is added to an R.DBMS structure, two classes of 'column' may be used - a fixed length field of, typically 64 or 256 characters maximum; and a variable length field of effectively unbounded length. Figure 7.2 shows a typical structure for library catalogue and stock records. There is a technical problem, of which the user should not normally be aware, in setting up the most efficient form of storage for variable length records, and this varies from one product to another. Some of the options available to the designer are :

•   Store all of the text within the relational tables, and allow the file handler to cope with the variable record lengths - a good solution if the texts are fairly short, and not too variable in length;

•   Store the variable length text fields as separate, but simplified and compressed rows or subfiles - good for space efficiency when text is really variable, but tends to lose presentation options (like word processor mark-up) and use more disc accesses;

•   Store the variable length text fields as separate, word processor format subfiles - good for editing and presentation, but even more likely to consume resources;

•   Some combination of the above, with options to select which method will be applied to each case on its merits - which may need a fair amount of technical know-how about the software.

The text 'columns' are then parsed and indexes formed of words in the text in an inverse file structure similar to that described for the text database systems. Because of the subdivision inherent in the R.DBMS columns, the pointers from the inverse file are simpler than for full text equivalents.

Some well established products (1988) :

INFOText - Doric (UK) & Henco Inc
INMAGIC - HEAD (UK) & Warner Inc
MINISIS - Assyst (EUR) & IDRC (CAN)

... and some making their mark :

DM - Information Dimensions
INFO-DB+ - Henco Software Inc.
SQL*TEXT - Oracle Corporation

A simple operation on the two tables of Figure 7.2 is shown in Figure 7.3, expressed in the SQL language, and the resultant 'shelf list', sorted in location order, forms Figure 4. The examples are drawn from Ashford (1987b), a study of the design for text extensions to ORACLE; they would, in practice, apply with little modification either to INFO-DB+, or to an SQL interface to DM.

Figure 7.3 : SQL commands in use

The shelf list table is formed by the
following operation on the Catalogue
(CAT) and the Locations (LOCN) tables :

SELECT	Location,ISBN,Copy,Author
FROM	CAT, LOCN
WHERE	CAT.ISBN = LOCN.ISBN
ORDER BY	Location,ISBN,Copy

Figure 7.4 : Shelf list from SELECT

Location	ISBN	Copy	Author
D:Z27	0-201-14502-2	2	Deitel, H M
R51	0-86238-091-X	1	Oxborrow, E A
Z225.9	0-201-19215-2	1	Date, C J
Z225.9	0-201-19215-2	2	Date, C J
Z225.9	0-201-19215-2	3	Date, C J
Z225.9	0-86238-091-X	2	Oxborrow, E A
Z276	0-201-14502-2	1	Deitel, H M
Z678.9	0-442-31770-0	1	Burton, P F ...

The dialogue might either be entered from a terminal, making use of a suitable interactive interface, or, for repeated similar searches, embedded in a compiled application program. Compilation may beneficially affect run time performance. In an interactive - and so interpretative - mode the command optimiser, which picks the best order to use indexes and refer to the source tables, must do the best it can step by step, whereas in a compiled program it has more opportunity to deal with a group of tables using overall database statistics. In larger systems, or where performance is critical, the assistance of an experienced programmer is essential.

Figure 7.5 shows a number of other SQL based searches, in interactive mode, chosen from other application areas. Figure 7.6 illustrates both a non-SQL language, which is well liked by users and easy to learn, and the way in which quite a complex function is embedded in a program so that the user has only a simple conceptual task. Replies to prompts for 'Project number' and 'Phase number' followed by a free text search string deliver a formatted table of project progress reports.

Figure 7.5 : SQL text retrieval from R.DBMS+Text

The following examples show extensions to SQL which have been used in the design of SQL*TEXT for one R.DBMS product. (Ashford, 1987b)

Text retrieval elements are in **bold**.

A 'personnel data' example

```
SELECT   ENAME,JOB,SA
FROM     EMP
WHERE    JOB = 'MANAGER'
AND      SAL > 28000
AND      REVIEW CONTAINS ('SATISF*' OR 'EXCELLENT');
```

The department staff table found in all R.DBMS manuals . . .

```
SELECT   DNAME,ENAME,JOB, SAL,LANGUAGE
FROM     EMP, DEPT
WHERE    EMP.DEPTNO = DEPT.DEPTNO
AND      LANGUAGE CONTAINS ((('ENG*' OR 'FRENCH') OR
         ('CJK' NOT 'KOREAN')) AND ('FLUE*' OR 'GOOD'))
ORDER BY      DNAME,SAL,DESC;
```

Selection from a maps catalogue

```
SELECT   MAPID,NAME,SCALE,TYPE,DATE
FROM     UKCS
WHERE    SCALE < 1,000,000
AND      SCALE > 50,000
AND      TYPE CNS(('SOLID' OR 'SUBSUR*') NOT 'DRIFT')
AND      COUNTRY CN ('UK' OR 'NORWAY')
AND      NAME CN (('VIKING' OR 'CEN*') AND 'GRABEN')
ORDER BY      NWY,NWX;
```

Although in any one example the search criteria tend to be fairly simple, the repertoire from which they are chosen is extensive. The major extension is in the availability of inverse file Boolean searching within the **CONTAINS** clause. **CN** appears to be becoming an accepted short form.

Search terms are enclosed in quotes to reduce complexities in the parser. The asterisk * is used to allow right truncation, to remove plurals etc. or merely to save typing long words.

47

Applications using R.DBMS + text

Several groups of applications are beginning to establish themselves for the R.DBMS + Text products, either dealing with the annotation of basically numeric data, or alternatively, managing structured text with data content.

In **accounting applications**, text fields may be added to standard relational records to allow the addition of explanatory comments, or the use of flexible product descriptions. Searches are made to find *'all subsidiary operations where value of the pound sterling has been cited in explanation during 1985'*, or *'consultancy services not separately charged'*.

Market research data, as presented, typically consists of numbers of tables - subsets of a large, sparse data matrix - with row by row commentary, and text bodies commenting on each table as a whole. On a database, the matrix may be held entire, with the annotative text either presented when sub-tables are selected, or used as part of the selection process. Searches using text might include *'only those responses described as significant'* or *'classes described as "impulse buyers" or "impulsive" or "unpredictable" or ...'* or *'free comments including the words "attractive" or "pretty" or "chic" etc..'*

Bibliographic records are records used to identify documents held 'elsewhere', as paper records, microform, or on optical discs. Figures 7.2 and 7.4 show an example of this widely used application. Searches might be made for *'all references to sea water or seawater or saline corrosion since 1982 published in English where the title includes stainless steel or (stress and austenitic)'*; *'all books by Samet on quad trees'*; *'references to magneto-optic effects in the keywords field, or either Kerr or Pockel in author or title fields'*. **Map catalogues** present a good application, since in addition to structured text fields , they add geographic coordinates, scale, geographic area codes (numeric), projection etc., all of which do not work too well under conventional free text databases. Similar comments apply to **control of drawings** for engineering projects, and **registry management** for conventional filing.

An appealing, but as yet (mid-1988) unproven application, would be to use an R.DBMS + Text database as the index to an optical disc-based document image store. The availability of free text indexing provides both flexible search and retrieval on profiles or abstracts taken from the documents, or, in the more advanced systems, the scanners can deliver parts of the image of the document in ASCII form by optical character recognition directly. At the same time, the R.DBMS processor should offer transaction restart following transient faults, and efficient and reliable 'rollback' to recover from more serious malfunctions - both of which are very desirable in an office environment with frequently accessed material. These are often more easily set up than in the free text systems.

Figure 7.6a : R.DBMS+text from a program context (INFOText)

```
PROG    PRINT-PG
REM         This program provides a formatted listing for any phase of a project, limiting the content
REM         of the report to selected activities. The text associated with the master file contains
REM         semi-structured and unstructured data. Activities are defined in Thesaurus entries, and
REM         the user may scan the concordance using wild-card searches to ascertain which words
REM         may be included in the Thesaurus entries.
REM
FORMAT    $NUM1,7,7,I              ; Time accumulator (used in other searches)
FORMAT    $NUM2,3,I                ; Phase number as input for search
FORMAT    $NUM3,2,I                ; Screen line number counter
FORMAT    $CHR4,8,C                ; Project number as input for search
FORMAT    $CHR5,79,C               ; ASEL or RESEL search command input
FORMAT    $NUM15,2,I               ; Work register
OUTPUT PROJECT-REPORT INIT         ; Initialise print output file
SELECT PROJECT-MASTER              ; Selects existing project data file
DISPLAY =                          ; Clears screen
DISPLAY AT 1,18, 'NEW PRODUCT DEVELOPMENT'
DISPLAY AT 2,18, '                                  ;
DISPLAY AT 4,1,      'Please enter Project Number'   ; Take in user data to select project
ACCEPT  AT 4,40,$CHR4
RESEL BY PROJECT = $CHR4                             ; Scope of selection is now chosen project
DISPLAY AT 22,1, 'You have ',$NOSEL,' records'       ; Tell user (system) count of records for this project
DISPLAY AT 5,1,      'Please give Phase Number'      ; Call for phase within project
ACCEPT  AT 5,40,$NUM2
RESEL FOR PHASE = $NUM2                              ; Scope of selection is now chosen project, phase
DISPLAY AT 22,1, 'You have ',$NOSEL,' records'
MOVE 'X' TO $CHR5                                    ; Forces at least one iteration
```

(continued in figure 7.6b)

49

Figure 7.6b : R.DBMS+text from a program context continued

```
CALC $NUM3 = 11                    ; Set screen line number
DISPLAY AT 8,1,      'Please enter text search required'
DISPLAY AT 9,1,      'Use "ASEL" with search words to extend the retrieved set'
DISPLAY AT 10,1,     'Use "RSEL" with search words to reduce the retrieved set'
DO WHILE $CHR5 NE ' ' AND $NUM3 LE 20    : Set up loop for user instructions
    MOVE ' ' TO $CHR5
    ACCEPT AT $NUM3,1,$CHR5            ; Read the text selection input in simple form
REM    Now increment the line number
    CALC $NUM15 = $NUM3
    CALC $NUM3 = $NUM15 + 1
    IF $CHR5 NE ' '
        EXECUTE $CHR5                 ; Make the requested search
        DISPLAY AT 22,1, 'You have ',$NOSEL, records'
    ENDIF
DOEND                                 ; Closes search loop
PRINT 'PHASE ',$NUM2,' ESTIMATES
PRINT '***************',
PROGRAM SECTION 2                     ; This is the output section
IF COM-FN = ' '                       ; COM-FN is an indicator in the data record
    PRINT *L1,TOPIC,COMMANDS,ESTIMATED-TIME,' days',
         *L1,*TEXT,SUGGESTION,*L1,'Originated by ',SB,
         *L1,'-----------------------------------------------',
ELSE
    PRINT *L1,TOPIC,COMMANDS,ESTIMATED-TIME,TIME,' days',
         *L1,*TEXT,COMMENTS,*L1,'Originated by ',SB,
         *L1,'-----------------------------------------------',
ENDIF
PROGRAM END
```

(INFOText Revision 9 users may care to try it out!)

Figure 7.7 : The pros and cons of DBMS and inverse file systems

DBMS : Strong features

Robust, efficient data structures
Control through data dictionary
Fast, efficient updating of fixed
field data and indexes
Individual users may have their
own 'views' of shared databases
Comprehensive restart and other
recovery procedures
User interface can include menus,
prompts, validation on screen

DBMS : Limitations

Usually must be embedded in programs
Interactive query languages often
need training and experience (eg SQL)
Requires computer specialist help in
setting up a system
Access points must be predefined and
change is not too easy later
Treatment of natural language texts
is an 'extra', and not widely available

FTX : Strong features

Natural language based, and good
at handling all aspects of text
Flexible and on-line user friendly
Minimum of computer specialist
assistance required, and system
is usually 'free standing'
Users can control the style and the
language of retrieval; thesaurus
gives control of usage and terms

FTX : Limitations

All users share the same view of
the text unless privacy codes or
other special arrangements are set
Addition of new data, and change to
existing records is expensive
Restart and recovery is usually based
on restore last dump and rerun -
warm restart is uncommon
Processing of numeric values is weak
relative to DBMS

Think about DBMS first for :

Structured data predominant
Mainly numeric or coded fields
Strong control of the user interface
Robustness to power supply or
equipment failures

Think about FTX first for :

Textual data predominant
Requirement subject to change
Flexibility of access points and of
user interface
Fast implementation or prototyping

. . . but remember . . .

Programmer assistance is likely
to be required in design and setup
Requirements should be clearly
defined before implementation

Databases should be reasonably stable
Changes should be mainly additions
Security and recovery need planning

Limitations

As with all relational database systems, the tasks of inserting and modifying data tend to use both central processor time and disc accesses fairly heavily. This is even more so with free format text, and care is necessary in designing both the structure and the user interfaces of systems in excess of 20 million characters of input data and text. For mainly reference (that is, 'read only') use, this is, of course, not a problem, as updates can be scheduled out of office hours or overnight.

Dealing with text in revisable form (RFT) from office automation systems or typesetting may be awkward in all systems. Only recently have functions to preserve mark-up[1] from word processing become available as standard facilities, and this should be approached carefully in applications where it is important as matching up database software and text processor is critical. The way in which one particular software developer has approached this issue is described in chapter 8.

Figure 7.7 summarizes the relative strengths and weaknesses of DBMS and inverse file approaches.

---

[1] mark-up : the extra characters inserted by word processors and computer typesetting systems to control format and style of presentation. In spite of current attempts at standardisation, they are still widely diverse in practice.

8 Design decisions for integration

In September 1987, Henco Software Inc.[1] released the first version of a new text and data management system, INFO-DB+, which extends, improves, and will presumably eventually replace, the earlier INFO and INFOText products. The second release was concerned mainly with fixes and performance enhancement, but by end-1988 a third 'stretch' version is scheduled, which will deliver additions to the functional scope of the new product. Since INFOText was not only the first successful *relational database + text* product, but has experience derived from more than 250 users in USA, UK and Canada, this provides a useful opportunity to examine the decisions made by the software designers as they committed the major part of the Henco's development resources to a rewrite of the 'flagship' product[2]. Most of what follows is concerned with the text acquisition, storage and retrieval features rather than the purely relational database side, but some aspects of the latter are significant also, as they were affected by considerations of database scale when text is involved, and of the market for minicomputer based systems.

INFO was first released on PRIME equipment in 1977 and by 1986 was a mature product running on PRIME, Digital Equipment (DEC) VAX and Data General, with an IBM-pc compatible version also. It had been built in to the database infrastructure and the user interfaces of the ARCINFO geographic information system by ESRI (Environmental Sciences Research Institute, Redlands, CA), and had also acquired one or two special purpose compiled versions to achieve faster performance than the basic software which was predominantly interpretative. Applications are written in a language unique to INFO (figure 7.6) and although this proved flexible, easy to use, and very fast for development work in the hands of skilled users, by 1987 it was a long way, in style and method, from the SQL based interfaces which had meantime become widespread. The way in which magnetic disc files were handled varied from one hardware version to another, relying on the hardware manufacturer's proprietary file systems, and lacking a fully portable implementation optimised for INFO processes. Much use was made of the technique of bit mapping to represent the scope of retrieved sets of results - which is fast and flexible, but essentially a small system methodology when judged by present day database size expectations (cf chapter 12).

INFOText was a joint development by Doric in UK and Henco in North America, in response to the developing acceptance of the full text retrieval

---

[1] and, some months later, Doric Computer Systems in UK

[2] Approximately 450,000 lines of C language code were involved.

systems, but in this case designed for a relational environment.[1] Mainly, though, it was a graft of a set of text management functions on to the existing INFO structure, and while it works well, and has sold well, its hybrid nature has always been apparent. (This 'bolt-on' approach was also followed in the later, 1987, design for ORACLE+Text shown in the examples in figures 7.2 to 7.5, partly so that ORACLE users could, if they wished, access the intermediate tables within the standard language.) Hybrids of this sort are easier to implement, but tend to lead to performance problems on larger databases as the frequently used routines are difficult to optimise.

When INFO-DB+ was being designed, the following requirements were established, based on experience with INFO and INFOText, and on feedback from users and market research :

- The primary development would be on DEC VAX equipment; others, including UNIX versions would follow as justified;

- Data and text acquisition, storage and processing would be integrated into a single working environment;

- Data in standard system files, and text in word processor files would be accessible to the INFO-DB+ databases directly;

- Existing applications in traditional programming languages (3GLs) such as COBOL, FORTRAN, C etc., should be able to use the database routines with minimal adaptation;

- Databases with text storage in excess of 1,000 million characters would be expected, and should perform efficiently for the user.

Certain design decisions flowed directly from these requirements. The use of bit maps for retrieved set representation was discarded as unlikely to sustain the expected database volumes. The distinctive INFO high level programming language was replaced by a new 'intuitive query language' - IQL. This is an SQL-like user language based on the primary commands :

SELECT <filename>   (*files* not *tables*)

RELATE <filename>   (to *join* another file)

RESELECT for <conditions>   (including *text* selection)

ASELECT for <conditions>   (to add records to the current set)

LAYOUT <contents, position> (to specify presentation formats)

LIST   (to display results)

---

[1] Its text features resemble STATUS in many ways - but this is not too unusual, as by 1983 the main styles were well established, and MIRABILIS and SIFT (a Norwegian package) appear to follow the same lead also!

SQL was not used in the primary versions because of its lack of text retrieval in context features, and its implicit limitations on the use of operating system file managers. In figure 8.1, user and program interfaces are shown in the upper part of the diagram, and information storage and gateways to other database systems in the lower part.

Figure 8.1 : INFO-DB+ design plan - 'stretch' version

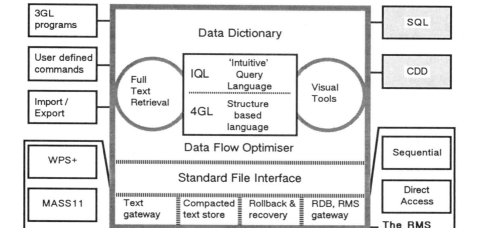

The *data flow optimiser* is the logical 'back end[1]' of the INFO-DB+ kernel, where decisions are made about the best strategy for record retrieval from diverse data resources; the *standard file interface* makes all of these sources look and behave similarly for the data flow process, so that the user or programmer (if the 3GL interface is used) need not be aware of the local formats or conventions. RDB is the DEC relational database product, and CDD the data dictionary from the same supplier. These are important for future *database* flexibility, but do not, in the short term, affect text capabilities.

---

[1] front end : between the user and the system proper; thereafter back end came to mean between the main processor and its data storage resources.

Planning the text functions

Major decisions which do affect text, however, were that most interactions would take place either through user dialogues in IQL, or through interfaces embedded in COBOL, FORTRAN, 'C' (3GL) or, in due course, 4GL programs. Secondly, that *either* revisable text - from word processors or desk top publishing systems - *or* a more compact, efficient internal format, *or both* would be required, for the application designer to choose.

The text gateway, and the set of revisable text products envisaged for the DEC VAX environment are shown in the lower left corner of figure 8.1. All text files may be processed by the parser, and inverse files and pointer lists built up in the usual way, concorded at either document, paragraph or word in sentence level, and subject to either stop word or go word limitations.

There was then a design choice about the format and presentation of the compacted text store. Most word processors offer a wide range of presentation options including multiple founts and sizes; bold, italic and underline; indentation and justification. (Some, like MacAuthor on which this text was prepared, and Microsoft Word, offer embedded graphics, in line formulae, footnotes, half-tone backgrounds and other options!) Now, while each product has its own presentation method for its own display, the prospect of developing a general purpose screen driver to offer wysiwyg[1] facilities for a number of diverse word processors is somewhat daunting. Conversely, the use of a simple ASCII text representation on screen loses much of the value of the format structure of the word processor document.

The decision taken was that users for whom exact presentation was important could choose to store the original text file, and call the specific word processor through an INFO-DB+ gateway when a display was required. There is then the option either to retain only these 'original' files, or to hold the compacted text also, for faster, simpler display. (Disc space is cheap - and, in real terms, becoming cheaper!) Other users might choose to use the compacted text store mainly, or exclusively, and for them a compromise format was developed. Each compacted file is accompanied by a descriptor record, in which those format effects which can effectively be delivered on a general purpose terminal and a standard driver are retained, notably bold, underline, indentation and tab settings. This allows reasonable presentation of normal texts and of tables, but in a single fount and size. Note that if the word processor text is retained, and the compacted text discarded, then the user has a more general purpose form of the word processor file search products currently being marketed for micro computers (eg. Gofer, Zy Index); also that in this DEC VAX environment, use of WPS+ implies the All-in-1 office environment.

---

[1]   wysiwyg = 'what you see is what you get'

Next phase developments

The current version is in the hands of users, existing INFO and INFOText sites are converting to INFO-DB+, and the effective handling of large text databases (around 1,000 million characters, or 1Gb) is demonstrable. What, then, has been deferred to the 'stretch' version, and is now seen by the designers as high priority?

Field types

First are the text field types present, and well liked, in INFOText, (and also included in ORACLE*Text) but left out of early releases of INFO-DB+. These are the fixed length, within the relational row, text field (the 'C' item in INFOText) and the variable length, but wholly internal rather than word processor generated text field (CX type). Both of these are sub-sets of individual relational records, rather than the document records characteristic of the implementation so far, and are, on the whole, related to indicative text (ITX) rather than full text applications (chapter 5). The likely choice will be to implement a dual purpose, more versatile CX type in INFO-DB+.

SQL and RDB

Implementation of an SQL alternative to IQL, and as a gateway from existing programs is important[1], and it may also be desirable to provide a general 'way in to INFO-DB+' from database products such as DEC RDB, which are well established but lack text facilities. This 'use anything, talk to anybody' design intention is a valuable open system objective, but not always easy to incorporate at a reasonable cost.

Extensions in the parser

Next comes the refinement of sentence identification, and more reliable treatment of punctuation exceptions. This will allow both proximity searching *across* sentence endings as an option, and also improve treatment of search phrases like "M'Nab & O'Connell v. McLean & ffoliot". Some design effort is also going in to provision of an interactive thesaurus capability - which at present depends on somewhat *ad hoc* implementations, maybe coupled to automatic identification and selective treatment of phrases in the parsing stages. More word processors may be required to be accommodated, and functional extensions to deal with document assembly - a *publishing* facility - and to incorporate pictures, line graphics and formulae are seen to be important. The report writing features of relational databases are flexible and convenient, but when text is incorporated among data fields, there are numerous problems to be solved in finding the best formats, and causing least work in specification.

---

[1] Final design decisions await the outcome of apparently complex discussions on an agreed standard for context-based retrieval within the SQL syntax.

Performance

Performance aspects which may be expected to get further attention are the further speeding up of *delete* processing - always a problem area in full text systems - and the ability to re-concord individual documents or document sets. Run-time-only, and read-only versions are also being evaluated.

No software is ever finally complete until it is obsolete, and the developments recorded here are only interim stages in the evolution of a complex product. It is, however, useful to be able to see the paths taken in radical revision of an early relational + text system, by a software company with some years in the marketplace and a reasonably successful sales record.

9 Optical disc storage systems

Previous chapters have dealt with total information projects based on proven technology and straightforward, if sometimes large scale, applications. The next five are concerned with what may be at least as important soon, beginning with a brief review of optical disc storage systems. This is a developing technology, and what follows may quickly become superseded. For those who wish to pursue the subject in more detail, the most comprehensive and readable technical introduction is still Hendley (1985), and his follow-up articles in *Information Media and Technology.* References to other useful periodicals will be found in chapter 15.

Optical disc storage presents the current major opportunity to extend the total information system, as it offers very large, reasonably fast, random access storage for encoded (ASCII or EBCDIC) text, vector graphics, digitized raster images, and both digital and analogue audio and video storage.

The optical disc

An optical disc consists of a flat disc of (usually) polymer, coated first with a metallic layer, and then with a protective varnish. It may be 12cm., 30 cm., or larger in diameter. The storage of digital data, or digitised analogue data as in the digital audio products, takes the form of a concentric or spiral arrays of fine pits in the metallised surface. In mastered discs, these are copies, made by pressing or injection moulding, of a laser etched master disc. Write once discs are sold as blank platters, and are written by lasers in the computer peripherals to which they are attached. In both cases the digitised data is read by measuring the intensity of a reflected laser beam which has been accurately aligned with the track of pits in the disc surface. The necessary precision engineering, the control of error rates and reconstruction of damaged data, and the production of many cheap reliable copies of master discs have represented considerable technical achievements. The erasable optical disc uses a different technology, and is potentially rather an attack on the high volume end of the magnetic disc range for data processing applications than a large, cheap storage device in itself. There is also some doubt as to whether it can achieve the ten to twenty year archival life expected from the write once optical discs.

CD-ROM[1] discs look like audio compact discs, use the same mastering and cheap reproduction technology, and hold up to 600 million characters (600Mb) of encoded text. CDI is an equivalent disc storing text, sound and (a few) visual images. Digital optical discs (ODs or DODS) of 30 cm. diameter or larger, are similar, except that they cost more to make, but they hold 2,000 Mb now, and will reach 4,000 Mb soon. Once pressed both CD-ROM and ODs are fixed, and cannot be updated - compare with gramophone records. WORM[2] discs come in similar physical sizes, have rather less than one half of the capacity for a given size, but can be written, once, from a computer peripheral drive, and then read many times - hence WORM. Each copy of a WORM must be written individually - compare with cassette tapes.

Text based systems

All of the main total information management products either have, or soon will have 'text on optical disc' capability, from micros to minicomputers, and mainframe systems are really only waiting for optical disc technology to be fully implemented for them also. Similarly, most of the commercial 'information providers', already have optical disc (usually CD-ROM) alternatives to going on-line, and it looks as if these products will proliferate rapidly, at least for material where being 'up to the minute' is not a major concern.

A well prepared commercial product is Whitaker's British Books in Print, now on CD-ROM as the BOOKBANK Service. A standard MS-DOS pc with 640 kb memory and a suitable CD-ROM reader may be used to access over 480,000 titles from 12,000 publishers. A 'CD-ROM specialised' version of BRS/SEARCH is used to access any word in the book records - author, title, publisher and so on, and a choice of five standard formats is available for the results. 'Gateways' include direct access to book ordering systems using telecommunications lines.

In the Netherlands, Kluwer Datalex has developed an IBM PC based approach using CD-ROM to distribute some of their range of specialist legal handbooks; this product uses the 'read only' version of microSTATUS. The 'adaptations' necessary in these two applications include dealing with the relatively slow access times of the compact disc, and with the large text and index volumes held on the dense medium. WORM products, which can be updated by writing further text until the disc is full, are also appearing using the same micro with adapted software to access the full text - another Dutch publisher, Samsom Veldkemp was an early user.

The Datext service (Datext Inc., Woburn MA) has been providing commercial information on CD-ROM since January 1986. It includes material from several information sources, including stock price and volume data;

---

[1] CD-ROM : Compact Disc - Read Only Memory

[2] WORM : Write Once, Read Many times!

company information; and biographical information on executives. Updated discs - four in all - are supplied every month, and superseded versions may be kept as an archival record. In library use at Dartmouth College (Fries and Brown, 1987) it was found to be of value as an integrated source for large amounts of recent data, especially by end-users who did their own searching, but this did not replace on-line searching for the most current material.

The US Patent and Trademark Office maintains an optical disc file of all US patents since 1975 - over 7 million of them - and this can be searched from remote terminals using a text retrieval system similar to that of the DIALOG on line service. So far only text is available, and access to diagrams etc. needs the original paper records.

At the micro end of the scale, Hitachi offers a CD-ROM drive for MS-DOS micro computer systems at about £750, but there are many problems of device, cable and operating system compatibility to be solved before these products can be regarded as routine plug-in options. Apple has produced a CD-ROM reader for the Macintosh at about $1,200, and already compatible electronic publishing products such as dictionaries, using hierarchic access systems like Hypertext and Guide are being marketed! For large scale, simply structured text products this approach appears to be practical, although once the subject matter is no longer effectively self-indexing the difference between basic tree structured access and real full text retrieval becomes evident. 'Tell me the meaning of "system", please' is easy - a simple index of dictionary head words will do. However, 'Show me the words in the dictionary which use "system" in the definitions' requires full text access capability. Standards are good for CD-ROM (the so-called High Sierra formats); weaker for text on larger discs, and as yet hardly started for digitised images.

Text plus images

Storage of digitised images in raster form, that is, as an array of black or white dots, takes much more space than encoded text. Compared with the 2,500 characters on a page of closely typed A4, a scanned image, even compressed, needs 50,000 bytes, and half-tones or colour images take much more again. While there are some systems which handle images in raster format on magnetic disc - and the Chicago public transport information system is a good example - it is the optical disc which has made the volumes generally acceptable. When text and images combine to form an integrated information presentation, the use of an indicative text system (chapter 5) to retrieve and present the dual solution is flexible and not too difficult to implement.

The main problems arise from the graphics quality required at the user terminal where a density of at least 30 points / cm. or 100 points / inch is the minimum for a decent quality of reproduction - and the large data volumes involved whenever a file is moved, compressed or de-compressed, or translated into a display or laser printer representation. Micro computer implementations usually need additional memory (up to 10 or 12 Mb in some cases), special compression / de-compression boards, and fast printer drivers. Most practical systems with more than a single user are based on local area networks (LANS), using Ethernet or a similar domain to get enough transmission capability. Wide area linkages are still a real problem, and only facsimile (Group IV) is being offered as a partial solution so far.

Raster images of text have, in themselves, no access point for a text retrieval processor, and it is necessary either to add keyword fields, or document profiles as used in office automation, or, working but not yet widely used, to convert text parts of the image by an optical character recognition unit to equivalent encoded text form. Simple systems - single index value, like a personal identity number, or basic hierarchies, like classifications of micro-fossils supported by pictures - need only simple retrievers, and almost any competent database handler will do.

All hybrid systems, with text plus graphics or images, require some sort of gateway, as was described in Chapter 5, to allow control to pass from the text based user process to the non-text complement. Two styles may be found. Where hybrids are *ad hoc* structures - for access to a system editor, for working a table into a graph, or for routing retrieved text to a desk top publishing system - the gateway is often a direct call to the operating system to execute the dual process, given a transfer file. In the increasing number of vertical product implementations, however, where the hybrid system has a longer life, the gateway is often built in to the text process as a dedicated sub-routine. This is more robust, and usually faster, as advantage can be taken of application specific features. Such well established vertical implementations include insurance claims records; press cuttings libraries; electronic publishing such as classified catalogues; digitized cartographic images; and engineering documentation.

The Library of Congress, for many years a pioneer in text retrieval systems, is committed to a large and complex optical disc project, using Data General micros, IBM mainframes and the Library's own retrieval system. It will cover legislative texts, sheet music, maps, manuscripts and other holdings - so far it has gone 'live' for on-line access to scanned texts only. In time it will provide a browsing service on terminals in the offices of Members of Congress.

The Musée d'Orsay, in Paris, holds an important collection of all forms of creative art covering the period 1848-1914. In order to make the many non-exhibitable works of the period - monuments, fragile photographs and designs - accessible to the visiting public, it was decided to employ a range of audio-visual presentations of this material. An important component is the database of digital images, so far more than 12,000 items, which may be accessed from 16 consultation points, each with a keyboard and high resolution colour moniter. (The system is planned to take 100,000 items one day.)

The computer is a DEC VAX 750 mini cluster, and is connected to the terminals by an optical fibre network. BASIS software is used for search and retrieval, and for management of the auxiliary files involved, and also provides simple and responsive interfaces for the general public.

The Ulster Folk Museum has established an international centre for emigration studies, and is creating a database of historical records which will draw together relevant materials on Irish-American migration. STATUS is used on a DEC VAX minicomputer to retrieve the text parts of the records, and is linked to Xionics DIP-X image processing software running on PC workstations to handle images. In due course, it will be possible to send facsimile documents world wide over standard facsimile (Group 3) transmission.

It is no accident that these cases are drawn from museums and archives, because they exemplify the characteristics of a good digital image application, namely, stable records; necessary integration of image and text information; regular and varied use of the collection; and careful attention to the interfaces for both professional and occasional users. Projects being tried out now, and likely to go into use soon, differ widely in their applications, but share the same basic criteria. Criminal records; full patent specifications; engineering drawings; newspaper photo archives; training manuals; planning enquiry records; large scale maps of water, sewage and power systems; satellite images for land use and geological studies, are all being considered.

10 Research into retrieval processes

Limitations of Boolean searching

Despite the many technological developments which have taken place since the first mechanised retrieval systems were developed in the early Sixties, the searching techniques available to the user of a text retrieval system have changed very little since nearly all current systems are still based on the Boolean searching techniques described in chapter 3.

There are several problems associated with this retrieval mechanism (Cleverdon, 1984; Salton and McGill, 1983; Stibic, 1980). The first is that end-users are often unable to formulate good queries using the Boolean operators of AND, OR and NOT and require the assistance of trained intermediaries. A second problem is the lack of control over the size of the output produced by a particular query. Without a detailed knowledge of the contents of the file, the searcher will be unable to predict *a priori* how many records will be identified which satisfy the query. There may be several hundreds if the query has been phrased in very general terms, or there may be none at all if too detailed a query has been input. In both cases, the searcher will need to reformulate the query in some way and then to carry out a second search which may retrieve a more useful number of records. A third limitation of Boolean searching is that the retrieval operations result in a simple partition of the database into two discrete sub-sets - those records which satisfy the query and those which do not. All of the retrieved records are thus presumed to be of equal usefulness, and there is no mechanism by which they may be ranked in order of decreasing probability of relevance. Finally, there are no obvious means by which one can reflect the relative importance of different components of the query, since Boolean searching implicitly assumes that all of the keys have weights of either unity or zero, depending upon whether they happen to be present or absent in the query.

With the rapid increase in the use of text retrieval systems, more attention needs, therefore, to be given to the provision of facilities which would enable end-user searching to be carried out in a more effective manner. Two main approaches have been suggested. The first of these involves the use not of the Boolean model but of a completely different one, specifically that of best match searching, also known as nearest neighbour or ranked output searching. This involves the use of statistical information as the primary input to the retrieval algorithms (Salton and McGill, 1983; van Rijsbergen, 1979).

Alternatively, intermediary systems are being developed in which a sophisti-cated interface is used to facilitate the use of a conventional Boolean system by providing a variety of help and advisory facilities. This approach differs drastically from statistically-based models since work in this area is increa-singly making use of knowledge-based techniques, originally developed for research into artificial intelligence. These two contrasting approaches to text retrieval are discussed in this and the following chapter.

Best match searching

A best match search matches the set of query words against the sets of words corresponding to each of the documents in the database, calculates a measure of similarity between the query and each document, and then sorts the docu-ments into order of decreasing similarity with the query. A typical measure of similarity is the number of terms in common, the so-called coordination level search which has been advocated strongly by Cleverdon (1984). In such a system, the output from the search is a ranked list, in which those docu-ments having most terms in common with the query are at the top of the list, and are thus displayed first to the user. Accordingly, if sensible query terms have been selected, the first documents inspected will be those which have the greatest probability of being relevant.

The best match approach has several attractive characteristics. There is no need to specify Boolean interconnexions between the words in the query since the search requires just an unstructured list of keywords. There need be no problems associated with the volume of output produced, since the user can search down the list just as far as is needed. A quick, precision-oriented search may involve the inspection of only the first five or ten records in the ranked list while greater recall may be achieved by going further down. It is normally very easy to take term weighting information into account also when calculating the degree of similarity between the query and the records in the file. These weights may, moreover, derive from user judgements of re-levance for previously inspected output, and there is thus a mechanism avail-able for the automatic incorporation of relevance feedback information if a second search is required. The main limitations of best match searching are that it is less well suited than the Boolean model to the precise specification of complex, multi-faceted subjects or of synonym and phrasal relationships between words, owing to the lack of the OR and AND operators. For these reasons, hybrid systems have been suggested using retrieval algorithms poss-essing the characteristics of both Boolean and best match searching (Salton et al., 1983).

A best match search can be implemented very efficiently using an inverted file searching algorithm which involves the *addition* of the pointer lists corre-sponding to the terms in a query[1] (Noreault et al., 1977; Perry and Willett, 1983). The addition of the lists may be achieved as follows. When a docu-

[1] rather than their intersection, union or negation as in Boolean searching.

ment identifier is encountered for the first time in the pointer list corresponding to some query term, a counter is allocated to that document and set to one; this counter is incremented by one each time that that document is encountered in subsequent pointer lists. When all of the lists have been processed in this way, there will be a new list containing the identifiers of all of those documents which have at least one term in common with the query, together with the actual number of common terms for each such document. Thus, the calculation of all of the similarities will involve disc accesses for the pointer lists only, as would be the case in a conventional Boolean system. The additional overheads are the storage required for the cumulation of the matching terms, and the sorting of the final similarities (which is needed to generate the document ranking). The procedure may be generalised to allow for the weighting of query terms by incrementing the counters by the weight of each query term, rather than by one; in this case, at the end of the processing of the query lists, each counter will contain the sum of the weights for those terms that are common to some document and to the query. Once the best matching documents have been identified, they can be displayed to the user at the terminal.

Query processing

The input of a query to a best match retrieval system requires the user merely to input a natural language statement. This can be a sentence-like description of the topic of interest, a list of keywords, the text of a known document or some combination of these. Each of the words in the input is identified and compared with a stopword list containing some number, typically one or two hundred, of commonly occurring words that are unlikely to be of use for retrieval purposes. Thus, a query such as :

ANYTHING ON THE USE OF STATISTICAL TECHNIQUES FOR AUTOMATIC TEXT RETRIEVAL

would be processed by an indexing routine to yield the query keywords :

STATISTICAL TECHNIQUES AUTOMATIC TEXT RETRIEVAL

and a similar list of keywords would be used to represent each of the documents in the database. Query statements are generally quite terse, and thus any given keyword is likely to occur only once. If a document abstract, or full text, is available, keywords may occur several, or very many, times and the document representatives may thus contain not only each of the selected keywords but also their frequencies of occurrence in the database.

It will be seen that the query representative above consists merely of simple keywords, and thus loses semantic information resulting from the relative positions of words in a text.

For example, a

GARDEN PARTY

is not the same as a

PARTY IN A GARDEN

and there are thus none of the noun phrases which characterise many manual indexing systems, such as

INFORMATION RETRIEVAL or

DATABASE MANAGEMENT SYSTEM.

The automatic identification of phrases by linguistic techniques has proved extremely difficult and it is only recently that research into automatic natural language processing has led to the introduction of natural language front-ends to database management systems (Cercone and McCalla, 1986; Salton and McGill, 1983). There is now interest in the use of such techniques for indexing purposes, as in the study by Sparck Jones and Tait (1984) which uses a natural language parser to generate grammatically acceptable noun phrases from sentence-length natural language queries. These phrases can then be searched for in document abstracts, with the expectation that the presence of a query phrase will provide a more substantive indicator of document relevance than does the presence of just the constituent keywords. However, the experimental results to date are not sufficient to determine whether the sophisticated linguistic processing used does indeed result in increases in system performance, and it remains to be seen how such processing can best be employed in text retrieval systems[1].

Once the set of words representing a query or document has been identified, some means must be found of overcoming the variants in word forms which are likely to be encountered in free-text systems. These variants arise from several causes including the requirements of grammar like BIBLIOGRAPHY and BIBLIOGRAPHIC; valid alternative spellings, RECOGNISE and RECOGNIZE; antonyms, ABILITY and DISABILITY; and problems arising from mis-spellings, transliteration and abbreviation. There is thus a need for a conflation algorithm, a computational procedure which reduces variants of a word to a single form for retrieval purposes. Term conflation is normally carried out in on-line systems at search time using right-hand truncation as specified by the searcher, rather than by automatic means; however, some experience is needed if effective truncation is to be achieved.

The most common automatic conflation procedure is the use of a stemming algorithm, which reduces all words with the same root to a single form by stripping the root of its derivational and inflectional affixes. In most cases, only suffixes are stripped. While differing in detail, most of the stemming

---

[1] Trying to automate the index of this book did not go too well either!

algorithms which have been reported in the literature make use of a dictionary of common word endings, such as -SES, -ATION, -ING etc. When a word is presented for stemming, the presence of these suffixes is searched for at the right-hand end of the word. If a suffix is present, it is removed, subject to constraints which forbid, for example, the removal of -ABLE from TABLE or of -S from GAS. In addition, a range of checks may be invoked to deal with cases like the doubling of terminal consonants which occurs when the present participle is used, as with FORGETTING and FORGET, or in Dutch, MAN/MANNEN and MAAN/MANEN formations in plurals. A comparative survey of a wide range of conflation procedures is provided by Lennon et al. (1981) while a detailed implementation is described by Porter (1980).

Stemming is easy to implement and provides a highly effective means of conflating words with different suffixes. However, there are many other types of word variant which are likely to occur in free text databases, and there have been several attempts to provide conflation mechanisms for them. A very general approach involves the system calculating a measure of string similarity between a specified query term and each of the terms in the dictionary component of the inverted file, using for example a similarity measure based on the numbers of 3-character substrings[1] common to a pair of word stems (Freund and Willett, 1981). An analogous technique forms the basis for the Vocabulary Inverted File component of the TRIP retrieval software. An alternative approach to query expansion assumes that words, or stems, which occur frequently together in documents have some kind of semantic relationship with each other. Hence, if one of them is specified in a query, a useful system facility would be the ability to bring frequently co-occurring words to the searcher's attention. Such an automatic facility mimics in part the role of a thesaurus in a conventional retrieval system; the difference is that co-occurrence data is inherently statistical in character whereas the relationships in a thesaurus are constructed on a semantic basis.

Weighting of search terms and relevance feedback

Best match searching implies the calculation of some quantitative measure of similarity between the query and each of the documents in the file, the calculated similarities then forming the basis for the ranking. The most important component of a similarity measure is the the term weighting scheme which is used to allocate numerical values to each of the index terms in a query or a document to demonstrate their relative importance. There have been extensive experimental and theoretical studies of index term weighting schemes (Harter, 1978; Salton and McGill, 1983). Of particular importance has been the development of probabilistic models of information retrieval which have been successful both in improving the effectiveness of experimental document retrieval systems and in providing a firm theoretical basis

---

[1] trigrams, formally

for the use of many types of retrieval facility (Croft and Harper, 1979; Robertson, 1986; Robertson and Sparck Jones, 1976; van Rijsbergen, 1979). Most investigations have involved the development of methods for the weighting of query terms, with the documents being characterised by binary, that is, *present* or *absent,* indexing.

Sparck Jones (1972) introduced the concept of collection frequency, or inverse document frequency (IDF), weighting. This involves assigning weights to the terms in a query which are in inverse proportion to the frequency of occurrence of those terms in the collection of documents which is to be searched. The rationale behind this approach is that people tend to express their information needs using rather broadly defined, frequently occurring terms and any more specific, low frequency, terms are likely to be of particular importance in identifying relevant material. This is because the number of documents relevant to a query is likely to be fairly small, and thus any frequently occurring terms must occur in many irrelevant documents. Infrequently occurring terms, conversely, have a greater probability of occurring in relevant documents, and should thus be considered as being of potentially greater importance for retrieval purposes. These considerations lead to the use of a weight of the form[1]

$$\log N/N(I)$$

for some term I which occurs in $N(I)$ of the N documents in the collection. Tests with the IDF scheme show that it consistently gives results which are superior for best match searching to those resulting from the use of unweighted query terms, where all of the query terms are considered to be equal importance for retrieval purposes.

Once an initial search has been carried out, and the user has inspected a few documents and evaluated their relevance to the query, a relevance feedback search can be carried out in which the system uses the relevance judgements to calculate a new set of weights. Using probability theory and the assumption that the occurrences of index terms in documents were statistically independent of each other, Robertson and Sparck Jones (1976) were able to provide a theoretical rationale for the use of a term weight which involves the probabilities of a term occurring in a relevant and in a non-relevant document respectively. In practice, it is convenient to replace the probabilities by frequencies of occurrence. The suggested weight is of the form :

$$\log \{[R(I)(N - N(I) - R + R(I))] / [(R - R(I))(N(I) - R(I))]\}$$

for a term which occurs in $R(I)$ of the R relevant documents. This formulation assumes that full relevance information is available, i.e., that $R(I)$ and R are known for each term and query. To use the weights in a predictive sense,

---

[1]   The use of a logarithmic function has been justified on information-theoretic grounds since the inverse frequencies can be regarded as probabilities (Robertson, 1974) and also as a limiting case of probabilistic relevance weights (Croft and Harper, 1979; Robertson, 1986).

where complete relevance data is not available, an initial best match search is carried out using the IDF weights. The documents resulting from this search are displayed to the user one at a time in order of decreasing similarity to the query, and the user is asked to make relevance judgements on some small number, five or ten, of the top-ranked documents. These judgements are used to estimate R(I) and R, and hence to calculate the relevance weights, for each of the query terms. These weights are then used for the relevance feedback search, which should reflect the user's interests more closely than did the initial, IDF-based search. The feedback search can be iterated at will, although the user need not, of course, do so if sufficient relevant material is identified by the initial search.

The relevance weights can also be used to provide another effective method for query expansion. In a normal relevance feedback search, the relevance weights are calculated just for the terms specified in the original query. If the weights are also calculated for those terms occurring in documents judged as relevant, high weighted terms can be displayed at the terminal as proposed additions to the query for use in the second, relevance feedback search (Robertson, 1986). Yet another way of utilising the relevance assessments of the initial documents is to allow the user to specify one, or more, of the relevant documents as the basis for the second search. In this case, the original query terms are replaced by the terms representing the chosen document, thus offering the possibility of automatic browsing in the database. An example of such a system, which is extremely popular with users if it is implemented, is described by Wade and Willett (1988).

The INSTRUCT system

The operation of some of the retrieval strategies discussed in this chapter is illustrated by reference to INSTRUCT, an experimental retrieval system developed to demonstrate a range of statistical approaches for text retrieval to students of librarianship and information science. Given the query used above :

ANYTHING ON THE USE OF STATISTICAL TECHNIQUES FOR AUTOMATIC TEXT RETRIEVAL

INSTRUCT gives the response

THE CURRENT FORM OF THE SEARCH TERM LIST IS AS FOLLOWS :

1 STATIST (981)	2 TECHNIQU (1046)
3 AUTOMAT (389)	4 FREE (582)
5 TEXT (859)	6 RETRIEV (1939)

- where the non-trivial words have been stemmed using Porter's stemming algorithm (Porter, 1980) and where the the bracketed numbers denote the postings frequency in the file which is being searched, a set of about 26,000 titles and abstracts from the Library and Information Science Abstracts database. The user decides to find database stems that co-occur frequently with the stem AUTOMAT, resulting in the display :

OF THE 20 STEMS IN THE CLUSTER CONTAINING AUTOMAT 3 ARE ALREADY INCLUDED IN THE QUERY.

HERE ARE THE OTHERS:

1 ALGORITHM (138)	2 LINGUIST (190)
3 INDEX (1682)	4 SEMANT (131)
5 WORD (610)	6 LANGUAG (1120)
7 THESAURU (237)	8 TRANSLAT (359)
9 DOCUM (1824)	10 QUERI (208)
11 SEARCH (1961)	12 TERM (1311)
13 INPUT (388)	14 PROCESS (2760)
15 OUTPUT (350)	16 METHOD (1980)
17 NATUR (837)	

It will be seen that nearly all of the stems displayed do have some sort of re-lationship with the stem which is being used as the basis for the search. The user can include any of them in the query and then select new stems from the updated list as the basis for query expansion. After several further expan-sions :

THE CURRENT FORM OF THE SEARCH TERM LIST IS AS FOLLOWS :

1 STATIST (981)	2 TECHNIQU (1046)
3 AUTOMAT (389)	4 FREE (582)
5 TEXT (859)	6 RETRIEV (1939)
7 INDEX (1682)	8 DOCUM (1824)
9 SEARCH (1961)	10 QUERI (208)
11 TERM (1311)	12 ALGORITHM (138)
13 CLUSTER (84)	14 HIERARCH (106)
15 HIERARCHI (52)	16 AGGLOM (4)
17 BOOLEAN (77)	18 NEAREST (15)
19 NEIGHBOUR (32)	

At this stage, the user decides to carry out a best match search. In all, INSTRUCT identifies 8,772 documents having at least one term in common with the query. This number is, of course, quite huge when compared with the output of a conventional Boolean search; indeed, almost one third of the database has been considered by the retrieval algorithm. However, because of the ranking which has been carried out, only those at the top are likely to have a strong degree of relevance to the query. In this case, the searcher elects to inspect the first five document titles in the ranking; for each, the sys-tem requests an assessment of the relevance of the document that is being displayed - a requirement that may really need the display of the abstract in addition to the titles shown here.

1/ 1984 1523
MASQUERADE: SEARCHING THE FULL TEXT OF ABSTRACTS USING
AUTOMATIC INDEXING
RELEVANT ? (Y/N)   Y

2/ 1983 6684
IS CLASSIFICATION NECESSARY FOR RETRIEVAL?
RELEVANT ? (Y/N)   N

3/ 1985 1603
A NOTE ON THE USE OF NEAREST NEIGHBORS FOR IMPLEMENTING
SINGLE LINKAGE DOCUMENT CLASSIFICATIONS
RELEVANT ? (Y/N)   Y

4/ 1985 5396
EVALUATION OF CLUSTERING METHODS FOR AUTOMATIC DOCUMENT
CLASSIFICATION
RELEVANT ? (Y/N)   Y

5/ 1985 4121
A PRACTICAL STEMMING ALGORITHM FOR ONLINE SEARCH ASSISTANCE
RELEVANT ? (Y/N)   Y

The user then elects to modify the query by letting INSTRUCT identify potentially useful stems on the basis of the documents which have been judged
to be relevant. The twenty stems which INSTRUCT calculates to be the best
at discriminating between relevant and non-relevant material are :

EXTRACTED STEMS ARE :

1 HASH (7)	2 MATRIC (12)
3 STEM (33)	4 KEEN (15)
5 CRANFIELD (15)	6 MORPHOLOG (15)
7 LINKAG (40)	8 EVAN (17)
9 INVERT (45)	10 INVERS (21)
11 DISTORT (21)	12 WARD (26)
13 ANALOG (26)	14 TRUNCAT (31)
15 STAR (32)	16 MATRIX (38)
17 MIX (41)	18 VARIANT (44)
19 AMBIGU (50)	20 BROWS (54)

While some of these stems are clearly related to the query as currently
formulated, like WARD from Ward's clustering method, KEEN,
CRANFIELD and EVAN which are all document test collections, and words
like STEM and TRUNCAT, the user decides not to include any of them in
the query but, instead, to carry out a browsing search.

In response to this, INSTRUCT displays the documents which have been judged to be relevant, one at a time and the searcher chooses the document :

EVALUATION OF CLUSTERING METHODS FOR AUTOMATIC DOCUMENT CLASSIFICATION

as the basis for a search, or, more precisely, the stems in its title and abstract, rather than the original set of query stems. This browsing-type search results in the following ranking of previously uninspected documents :

6/ 1985 3237
HIERARCHIC AGGLOMERATIVE CLUSTERING METHODS FOR AUTOMATIC DOCUMENT CLASSIFICATION
RELEVANT ? (Y/N)   Y

7/ 1984 4930
APPLICATIONS OF MULTIDIMENSIONAL SCALING: COMMENT ON A METHOD FOR STUDYING INTERCORRELATED CIRCULATION PATTERNS IN LIBRARY SYSTEMS
RELEVANT ? (Y/N)   N

8/1983 3321
SOME METHODS OF CITATION ANALYSIS AND THEIR APPLICATION TO JOURNALS IN ENVIRONMENTAL/CIVIL ENGINEERING (IN JAPANESE)
RELEVANT ? (Y/N)   N

9/1983 5122
EXPERIMENTS IN LOCAL METRICAL FEEDBACK IN FULL-TEXT RETRIEVAL SYSTEMS
RELEVANT ? (Y/N)   Y

This document may now be used to initiate a new browsing search; thus, interesting documents identified in the course of one browse can then be used for further browsing searches. The search continues in this way, initiating new searches until the user is satisfied that this part of the database has been investigated in sufficient detail. At that point, all of the relevant documents identified in the course of the browse are noted, and a new set of potentially useful stems identified via the relevance-based query expansion routine as before. These could then be used to augment the current list of stems as a precursor to further searching using, for example, a relevance feedback search based on the original query terms together with those added from the list above.

It will be clear from this example that statistically-based systems provide a very wide range of retrieval facilities that differ markedly from those available in current Boolean systems; detailed discussions of those implemented in INSTRUCT are presented by Hendry et al. (1986a,1986b) and by Wade and Willett (1988).

11 Research into user interfaces

Retrieval systems such as INSTRUCT seek to overcome the limitations of Boolean retrieval by using a different type of retrieval algorithm. An alternative, and increasingly popular, way of improving on-line systems is to provide a front-end, or intermediary, computer system between the user and the search process (Keyhoe, 1985; Marcus, 1983). There are now many software packages available that provide pre-search query formulation and storage, automatic logon, downloading and menu-based interfaces. These are normally designed for use with micro computer equipment acting as terminals for on-line database hosts. While easier to use than basic command-based interfaces, such systems can only alleviate the inherent problems of Boolean retrieval. More advanced front-ends simulate a best match retrieval system or, more ambitiously, attempt to model the actions of a human intermediary using knowledge-based techniques originally developed for artificial intelligence research.

Simulation of best match searching

Here the interface is programmed to provide a best match interface to a public on-line database host that uses conventional Boolean retrieval algorithms. An example of work in this area is the **CIRT** system (Robertson et al., 1986) which provides a practical test bed for novel information retrieval techniques which have been tested extensively in laboratory environments but not under realistic conditions with user requests and real relevance judgements. CIRT runs on a front-end minicomputer which accepts natural language queries and allows best match searching of the Data-Star implementation of the MEDLINE[1] database. It uses both IDF and relevance weights[2]. The use of a public retrieval system requires a procedure for the conversion of a weighted term search into Boolean searches which can be processed by the host's retrieval software. The inverted file, best match search algorithm described previously assumes rapid access to the complete pointer lists for the query terms. This algorithm could be used only if these lists were downloaded to the front-end processor, a totally infeasible approach given the sheer size of the lists (unless extremely specific, infrequently occurring query terms were chosen) and the very restricted bandwidth of current data communications networks. Instead, an algorithm is used to generate a large number of Boo-

---

[1] MEDLINE : a major medical database of the National Library of Medicine, USA

[2] IDF : inverse document frequency and weighting (chapter 10)

lean combinations which, taken together in the appropriate sequence, result in the same output as a conventional best match search.

For example, consider a natural language query involving the three terms A, B and C and assume that an unweighted Boolean model search was being out. Then the sequence of three searches :

A AND B AND C

(A AND B) OR (A AND C) OR (B AND C)

A OR B OR C

will result in the production of all documents having three, two or one terms respectively in common with the query. This is an elegant idea but suffers from the very large number of Boolean combinations which need to be submitted to the host if anything but the shortest queries are to be searched against the database. CIRT uses a modified form of this procedure which minimises the number of combinations generated and submitted to the host and which also permits the weighting of the search terms. Documents are thus retrieved and displayed to the searcher in order of decreasing similarity to the query, using either IDF or relevance weighting.

Knowledge-based front-ends

Best match and related techniques use statistical information as the basis for the retrieval algorithms algorithms which are used. An alternative approach that has recently come to the fore involves the use of knowledge-based techniques derived from research into artificial intelligence. Such techniques have been applied to several areas of information science and we shall illustrate their utility for the implementation of two front-end systems, CANSEARCH and PLEXUS; these and other applications are discussed by Davies (1986), Smith (1987) and Vickery and Brooks (1987a, 1987b).

CANSEARCH

The CANSEARCH system is designed to facilitate end-user searching of the cancer therapy literature in the MEDLINE database (Davies, 1986; Pollitt, 1984). Like much of the medical literature, the terminology of this subject domain has been encoded in the Medical Subject Headings (MeSH), a hierarchical thesaurus used for indexing documents in MEDLINE. It maps naturally and readily on to hierarchically connected, menu-based computer interfaces and CANSEARCH uses this feature to provide a systematic way of leading end-users to those MeSH terms that best characterise their area of interest. The system is based on the premise that while searchers may not know exactly what terms they should use, they will certainly recognise them once they see them displayed. Users thus do not need to know how MeSH is constructed or how to use it; instead, appropriate sub-sets of the thesaurus are displayed at the terminal to allow them to choose those terms which apply to their current question. The user specifies a choice by touching a screen at the appropriate location; a new frame from the hierarchy is then presented that corresponds to the chosen subject. In all, there are 41 frames in the hierarchy, arranged into a total of seven levels, although only three or four are typically needed for the specification of a search. The terms displayed on a particular frame are either high level terms that need expansion, end-terms for searching MEDLINE or terms that would be translated into sub-headings for the modification of other terms and so on. The frame hierarchy provide a series of term choices which are used by the system to generate syntactically correct MEDLINE search statements that can then be submitted for searching. The operation of CANSEARCH will be illustrated by the frames displayed during the first part of a search for the query

CHEMOTHERAPY IN THE TREATMENT OF BREAST CANCER

The first frame displayed is shown in Figure 11.1; the user touches the item 'cancer at a particular site*' and the selection is indicated by reversing the video for the chosen string and redisplaying the frame.

Figure 11.1

frame 2		**PLEASE TOUCH A TERM OR CONTINUE**
all cancers	**OR**	cancer at a particular site*
		cancer of a particular histological type*
therapy*	**OR**	multimodal therapy*
patient details*		
miscellaneous concepts (eg recurrence, radiation induced . .)*		

* indicates further specification to follow
SELECT EVERY RELEVANT ITEM - ALL must be in document for retrieval

RESTART   NO SELECTION   CONTINUE

(In figures 11.1 to 11.5, **bold text** has been used to replace reversed video in selections, as well as for the original headings, since reversed video does not reproduce well in the illustrations.)

Figure 11.2

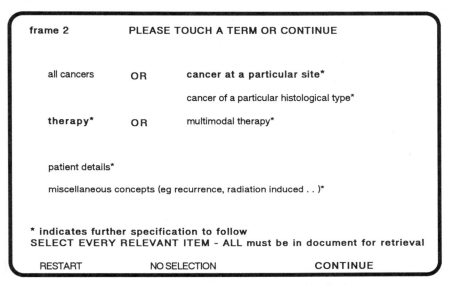

frame 2   **PLEASE TOUCH A TERM OR CONTINUE**

all cancers   **O R**   **cancer at a particular site***

cancer of a particular histological type*

therapy*   **O R**   multimodal therapy*

patient details*

miscellaneous concepts (eg recurrence, radiation induced . .)*

* indicates further specification to follow
SELECT EVERY RELEVANT ITEM - ALL must be in document for retrieval

RESTART   NO SELECTION   **CONTINUE**

A further selection is made, by touching 'therapy*', to complete the top level specification of the search topic as shown in Figure 11.2.

Figure 11.3

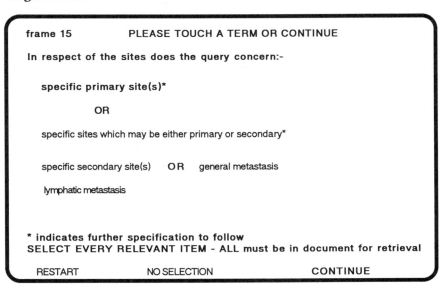

frame 15   **PLEASE TOUCH A TERM OR CONTINUE**

In respect of the sites does the query concern:-

specific primary site(s)*

OR

specific sites which may be either primary or secondary*

specific secondary site(s)   **O R**   general metastasis

lymphatic metastasis

* indicates further specification to follow
SELECT EVERY RELEVANT ITEM - ALL must be in document for retrieval

RESTART   NO SELECTION   **CONTINUE**

The frame shown in Figure 11.3 is displayed in response to the selection of 'cancer at a particular site*', and after selecting 'specific primary sites*' in Figure 11.3, 'breast*' is selected in Figure 11.4 to complete the specification.

Figure 11.4

```
┌─────────────────────────────────────────────────────────────────┐
│                                                                   │
│   frame 15a           PLEASE TOUCH A TERM OR CONTINUE             │
│                                                                   │
│                  as primary  /  as secondary                      │
│                                                                   │
│          abdiminal                   head and neck                │
│           peritoneal                 mouth*                        │
│            retroperitoneal           nervous system*              │
│          anal gland                  orbital                      │
│          bone*                       otorhinolaryngologic'         │
│          breast                      pelvic                       │
│          digestive system*           skin                         │
│          endocrine gland*             sebaceous gland             │
│          eye                          sweat gland                 │
│            conjunctival              soft tissue                  │
│            eyelid                    splenic                      │
│          choroid                     thoracic*                    │
│          facial                      urogenital                   │
│                                                                   │
│   * indicates further specification to follow                    │
│   SELECT ALL RELEVANT SITES - ANY one is sufficient for retrieval │
│                                                                   │
│   RESTART              NO SELECTION                CONTINUE       │
└─────────────────────────────────────────────────────────────────┘
```

The next frame to be displayed, Figure 11.5, is the top therapy frame and 'chemotherapy' is selected, leading to a sequence of frames that allow the specification of the particular drug of interest. Once the MeSH terms corresponding to the two parts of the query have been identified in this way, the system then generates a syntactically correct **MEDLINE** search statement.

Experimental tests of CANSEARCH have been carried out using real cancer therapy queries and doctors with little or no previous experience of on-line searching. The tests have shown that these doctors can, on occasion, produce better quality search formulations than can trained on-line searchers, although the latter show a better level of performance overall. The adequacy of the two sets of searches was assessed by experienced indexers from the MEDLARS section at the British Library Document Supply Centre. Thus, while CANSEARCH clearly cannot replace a trained searcher, it does allow end-users to carry out relatively effective searches for themselves if required to do so; similar comments probably apply to all of the experimental systems discussed in this and the previous chapter.

Figure 11.5

```
┌──────────────────────────────────────────────────────────────────┐
│  frame 3              PLEASE TOUCH A TERM OR CONTINUE              │
│                                                                    │
│         all treatment methods                                      │
│                                                                    │
│                     chemotherapy*                                  │
│                     cryotherapy                                    │
│                     diet therapy                                   │
│                     fever therapy                                  │
│                     nursing                                        │
│                     palliative treatment                           │
│                     prevention and control                        │
│                     radiotherapy*                                  │
│                     rehabilitation                                 │
│                     surgery*                                       │
│                                                                    │
│                                                                    │
│   SELECT ALL RELEVANT TREATMENTS - ANY is sufficient for retrieval │
│   * For detailed specification select ONLY the therapy concerned   │
│                                                                    │
│      RESTART            NO SELECTION                CONTINUE        │
└──────────────────────────────────────────────────────────────────┘
```

CANSEARCH uses two sorts of knowledge-based processing. Firstly, the subject knowledge of a trained indexer or intermediary is made available to the user by means of the MeSH displays, which thus function as a knowledge base to assist the inexperienced searcher. The equation of 'knowledge base' with a thesaurus is not inappropriate given a sufficiently sophisticated and developed thesaurus such as MeSH with its rich network of hierarchic and non-hierarchic term relationships. Secondly, the actual implementation is via a rule-based approach with a large number of rules covering the selection of frames, the processing of the results of the term selection, the generation of the search statements and the handling of the interaction with MEDLINE. The central feature of the system is the 'blackboard' which is divided into sections, or boards, which are consulted and updated by the rules as they are fired and which act as a record of the data captured during the course of a dialogue with a user. There are boards for the overall control of the system, and for the specification of the site, the type and the therapy of the cancer of interest, since a query will normally require the specification of one or more of these three types of concept. Blackboard-based systems are of increasing interest for the application of artificial intelligence techniques in information retrieval contexts owing to the need to integrate many different types of knowledge that may be required for the execution of a successful search (Davies, 1986; Croft and Thompson, 1988).

PLEXUS

The success of CANSEARCH is due in large part to the narrowly specific nature of medical terminology, the very restricted subject domain and the associated limited range of query types that need to be encompassed by the system. This domain specificity is characteristic of most successful applications of expert systems; more general domains are awkward to implement using knowledge-based techniques, and so the designers of the PLEXUS system set themselves a challenging task when they developed a system to simulate the intelligent behaviour of an intermediary in connecting a searcher with sources[1] which might be expected to satisfy the information need (Vickery and Brooks, 1987b; Vickery et al., 1987). Information needs are often expressed very roughly and a major part of the software in the system is concerned with fitting a natural language statement of the user's query into a framework which PLEXUS can 'understand' and analyse for completeness.

This understanding is based on semantic categories assigned to each word in the dictionary and is specific to the chosen domain of gardening. Having constructed a model of the problem statement, PLEXUS is able to use its knowledge of the way in which the model was constructed as the basis for the formulation of an initial Boolean query for searching against the database using an attached, and conventional text retrieval system. PLEXUS is thus basically an intelligent front-end interface to aid question formulation and modification.

Query formulation in PLEXUS involves restructuring the text of the user's input into units that represent the meaning of that text. This involves first stemming and then assigning a semantic category to each of the terms in the original input that do not appear on a stopword list. The meaning of a stem is identified by assigning that stem to at least one of a number of pre-established semantic categories which are specified in the system dictionary. The current version of PLEXUS supports eleven semantic categories (objects, parts, operations, processes, interactions, instruments, attributes, environments, use, time, locations) subdivided into a further forty sub-categories. The categories and sub-categories have been chosen to organise all the stems which might be encountered in questions and statements about the subject domain. Assigning a stem to one of these categories identifies the stem's meaning within the query with a view towards assessing the overall coherence and sufficiency of the query as a statement of the user's information need.

The PLEXUS dictionary contains all the stems that the system recognises; these stems have been drawn from a variety of sources, including the Broad System of Ordering (BSO) hierarchy (Coates et al., 1978) and a large number of sample queries taken from a popular book on gardening. Thus, there are many stems in the dictionary which cannot be used to index the ma-

---

[1] . . . in the form of documents, books, specialist organisations or individuals.

terial in the database directly but which might be found in a user's query. Over four hundred of the stems in the dictionary are associated in some two hundred semantic nets which link synonymous stems together, eg. the vernacular and Latin names for plants.

The meanings of query stems which are not found in the system dictionary are clarified through a simple question-and-answer type interaction with the user. So PLEXUS may ask questions like

IS OBJECT X A TOOL?

or

IS OBJECT Y A PLANT?

Such clarification dialogues are characteristic of natural language interfaces in a wide range of application areas.

Some of the stems in the dictionary might be assigned to more than one semantic category, e.g., PRUNE can be an action or an object. If such a stem is found in a query the most appropriate meaning is inferred by consideration of the semantic categories which have been assigned to other stems in the query. The system does so by making inferential use of contextual knowledge which is stored in the form of a series of pre-established structures specifying what combinations of semantic categories are likely to occur in a query. Thus PLEXUS tries to infer the meaning of a query by imposing a framework, or context, on that query which shows how its constituent stems relate to each other. A particular context is defined as a template specified by the number of stems present in the query statement, the semantic categories associated with these stems and the number of stems in a particular semantic category which are present. Eleven different templates have been identified in the prototype: ten of these were drawn up by analysis of 150 questions on gardening and the eleventh is a general framework intended to catch all cases which do not fit any of the other defined templates.

Once a context has been imposed on the query, PLEXUS builds a model of the query consisting of one or more interconnected frames, where each frame represents a significant term in the query and has a particular form and structure specific to a particular concept class. Frames are made up of slots into which appropriate information can be placed, eg. a term's BSO number or a synonym net pointer. It is not necessary for all the slots in a frame to be filled but before a search is executed PLEXUS will check each frame to ensure that enough is known about each concept to support the formulation of a suitable Boolean search strategy. Where insufficient information is available, the user will be prompted with a suitable question. This problem modelling stage is used to provide the information necessary for the production of an initial search strategy, which will consist of one or more stems linked by Boolean operators.

This Boolean query is then input for searching by MIRABILIS, a microcomputer text retrieval package developed at the University of London; the actual database of referral sources which is searched contains about 500 documents, organisations and individuals. The initial strategy is modified until an appropriate number of items has been retrieved, typically between one and ten items. The path chosen varies with the nature of the query but will typically start off with the ORing together of synonymous stems and the ANDing together of the resulting sets with the remaining individual stems. The initial search strategy thus formed might then be broadened or narrowed by entering related descriptors from the BSO classification, dropping existing query stems, adding synonyms of an existing query stem or by changing ANDs linking stems which occur in the same sub-categories to ORs etc. The precise way in which the query is modified is determined by a set of rules based on the encoded knowledge of the way the query has been constructed. For example, the dropping of stems is carried out using a ranking of the relative importance of the semantic categories available. When a suitable number of records has been retrieved by MIRABILIS, they are displayed for the user's consideration. References are presented to the user in what is considered to be the most appropriate manner possible so that, for example, institutions are presented in order of their distance from the user's home.

Applications

In this and the last chapter, we have described two alternative approaches to the further development of text retrieval systems. Of these, the statistical approaches based on best match searching have been studied for much the longer; the discussion in Chapter 10 above covers only some of the many techniques which have been suggested for use in best match searching and the reader is referred to the book by Salton and McGill (1983) for an extended discussion of this literature. The strengths and weaknesses of best match searching are now well understood and increasing use is being made of such techniques in operational systems of various sorts. IQ, an enhancement to the basic STATUS retrieval system, incorporates a procedure that uses relevance weights to rank all paragraphs in a database that contain at least one word or phrase in a user query. OKAPI uses automatic term conflation and best match searching in an on-line public access catalogue (OPAC) for the monograph holdings of the library of the Polytechnic of Central London. Both of these end-user systems are described in detail in a special issue of the journal Program (Vol. 22, part 1, 1988) that is devoted to non-conventional text retrieval systems; an analogous special issue is that of the journal Information Processing and Management (Vol. 24, part 3, 1988) while a general review of statistical retrieval methods is provided by Willett (1988).

General reviews of knowledge-based approaches to information retrieval are provided by Davies (1986), Keyhoe (1985) and Smith (1987). These have been developed more recently than the statistically-based approaches and operational systems are thus still quite rare. However, PLEXUS, which represents the current state-of-the-art in the use of expert system techniques to emulate an human intermediary, is now being marketed commercially for the searching of the INSPEC database under the name of TOME SEARCHER. Commercial implementations of CANSEARCH have not appeared yet, but this type of approach seems well suited to any application area where there is an established, hierarchically organised thesaurus that can be mapped readily on to a frame-based user interface.

The relative advantages and disadvantages of the knowledge-based and statistically-based approaches to text retrieval are being increasingly discussed (Salton, 1986) and there seems to be a coming together of these disparate approaches to document retrieval. For example, Croft and Thompson (1987) have described a system I^{3}R (the Intelligent Intermediary for Information Retrieval) that uses a range of language processing and expert systems techniques for the specification of the query and probabilistic best match searching techniques for the retrieval of documents from the database. A similar, integrated approach has been advocated as the result of a recent comparison of the retrieval performances of two of the systems discussed here, INSTRUCT and PLEXUS. This study demonstrated that the best results were obtained by using PLEXUS to process the user's initial query statement; the resulting query was then input to INSTRUCT for the actual search (Wade et al., 1988). It will be very interesting to see the extent to which these alternative sorts of retrieval system will complement or supplant the current generation of purely Boolean systems.

12 Text scanning alternatives

Early text retrieval systems were based upon the use of magnetic tape storage, with the data in serial files. This file structure offers several advantages for the implementation of large retrieval systems in that it is efficient in terms of storage, requires little processing, and accommodates new records by placing them at the end. Retrieval is based on pattern matching and requires the comparison of the words or stems comprising the query with the text strings representing each document in the file to determine whether these query words are present and whether the document satisfies any constraints specified in the query, such as logical or adjacency operators.

The obvious way to search for a particular string of characters (the pattern) in another string (the text string) is to place the pattern alongside the start of the text string and then to compare the first character of the query pattern with the first character of the text string. If these first characters match, the second characters are compared and so on until either a mismatch is found or the entire pattern is located. If a mismatch occurs between a pair of characters the pattern is shifted by one position towards the right end of the text string and the matching process is resumed starting at the beginning of the pattern[1]. This is clearly very time-consuming and a complete serial search of a large database is usually prohibitively inefficient using conventional hardware. Salton and McGill (1983) note that a search of a 1 GB[2] database using a computer system capable of processing 100,000 bytes per second would entail a response time of some 2.7 hours.

Increases in computer processing power and storage capacity, improvements in telecommunications, and reductions in the cost of direct access storage devices have led to the development of the interactive text retrieval systems which form the focus of this book. As described in Chapter 3, these do not exhaustively search their entire databases but instead use inverted file organisation to provide a sufficiently fast response for interactive searching. However, a considerable amount of additional storage is needed since the indexes are often comparable in size with the source documents in the main data file. A further disadvantage is the high computational overheads required for the generation and maintenance of the auxiliary indexes, as exemplified by the updating strategies described in chapter 5. In addition, it is often difficult to

---

[1] Note that the pattern does not really move as the necessary operations are carried out by maintaining pointers to the current locations in the pattern and in the text.

[2] 1 GB = one gigabyte = 1,000,000,000 characters - by no means uncommon in practice.

implement efficiently the pattern matching operations needed for certain types of request; examples of such facilities include left-hand truncation, variable-length don't care (VLDC) and embedded substring searches, like looking for antibiotics in a chemical database using the substring *MYCIN* (Kracsony et al., 1981; Freund and Willett, 1982). This sort of search can be executed only using full text scanning, despite the fact that such a scan is exceedingly slow, and quite inappropriate for online searching using conventional retrieval methods. There has accordingly been considerable interest in the development of new software and hardware techniques to improve the efficiency of serial text searching, as described in this and the next chapter. Two main techniques have been suggested to increase the efficiency of text scanning - the use of faster pattern matching algorithms and of text signatures.

Pattern matching algorithms

One of the disadvantages of the simple pattern matching algorithm described above is that the matching must restart at the beginning of the pattern many times and this can make the algorithm very inefficient. The worst case running time occurs if for every possible starting position of the pattern in the text, all but the last character of the pattern matches the corresponding character in the text, and it can be shown that in this case O(MN) character comparisons are needed to determine that a pattern of length M characters does not occur in a text string of length N characters.[1]

The theoretical analysis of such 'algorithmic complexity' is an increasingly important area of modern computer science (Weide, 1977). Although this O(MN) behaviour is rather unusual in practice, the simple algorithm also has the disadvantage that it may involve 'backing up', a re-positioning of the pointer to the current character in the text string; this may cause complications if the whole text string is not held in memory and buffering operations are necessary. However, more sophisticated string search algorithms have been developed that can search a text string for a given pattern in linear or even sub-linear time, where the number of character comparisons needed does not exceed the number of characters in the pattern and text strings. These algorithms involve a pre-search analysis of the pattern string or strings and the construction of auxiliary tables to control the character comparisons which are carried out (Aho and Corasick, 1975; Boyer and Moore, 1977; Knuth, Morris and Pratt, 1977; Smit, 1982). Two of these algorithms, those due to Boyer and Moore and to Aho and Corasick, are described below.

Unlike the simple algorithm, the algorithm due to Boyer and Moore (1977) compares the pattern with the text from the *right-hand end* of the pattern. Each time a match is found, a left shift is made until either the start of the pattern is reached, indicating that the pattern has been found, or a mismatch

---

[1] The notation O(X) denotes a computation, the average running time of which is directly proportional to X, the number of items that need to be processed (i.e., the number of characters in this case).

occurs. Whenever a mismatch occurs the pattern is shifted to the right by the larger of two pre-computed functions, $\Delta 1$ and $\Delta 2$, and the matching process resumed. $\Delta 1$ is a function of the text character at which the mismatch occurs and is equal to the shift necessary to achieve coincidence with the current text character if that character is also in the pattern. If, as is most commonly the case, that character is not in the pattern then $\Delta 1$ is equal to the length of the pattern. $\Delta 2$ is a function of the position in the pattern at which a mismatch occured. When a portion of the pattern has already been found to match some substring in the text, then if this substring also occurs again in the pattern $\Delta 2$ is the shift necessary to bring the new occurrence of the sub-pattern into coincidence with the matching substring.

The basic idea behind the Boyer-Moore algorithm is that more information is gathered by matching the pattern from the right than by matching from the left. In fact enough information can be gathered to determine that, without having to inspect them, some text characters cannot be part of an occurrence of the pattern in the text string and therefore can be skipped over. Thus, unlike the simple algorithm, the Boyer-Moore algorithm is usually sub-linear in nature, the degree of speed-up depending on the length of the pattern. For pattern lengths of six or greater the algorithm has been shown to be capable of out-performing search instructions built into the computer hardware (Horspool, 1980). For short patterns, less than about four characters, its performance is relatively poor and unless the pattern is found quite early in the text string, the simple algorithm is then usually preferable (Horspool, 1980; Smit, 1982).

The Boyer-Moore algorithm has an average time complexity of $O(N)$ but has a worst case running time of $O(MN)$; however, modifications of the basic algorithm have been suggested that reduce the worst case performance to $O(N)$. Horspool (1980) developed and tested a simplified version of the Boyer-Moore algorithm using only a single table, based in large part upon $\Delta 1$, which gives almost identical timings to the original form.

The operation of the algorithm is illustrated in Figure 12.1 with reference to the text string

DEVELOPMENTS IN PATTERN MATCHING ALGORITHMS

in which we wish to search for the truncated pattern ALGORIT*.

Figure 12.1 Boyer-Moore matching

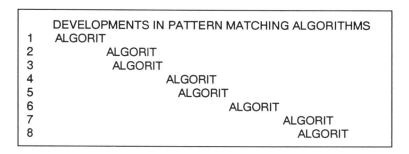

The execution of the search involves 8 stages as shown above :

1. The pattern and the text string are aligned and the last pattern character, 'T', is compared with the corresponding text string character, 'P'

2. 'P' does not occur anywhere in the pattern so the entire pattern is shifted to the right past the 'P'. The pattern 'T' is compared with the text string 'I'

3. 'I' occurs in the pattern which is accordingly shifted until the two 'I's are matched. The pattern 'T' is compared with the text string 'N'

4. 'N' does not occur anywhere in the pattern so the entire pattern is shifted to the right past the 'N'. The pattern 'T' is compared with the text string 'R'

5. 'R' occurs in the pattern which is accordingly shifted until the two 'R's are matched. The pattern 'T' is compared with the text string 'Δ'

6. 'Δ' (ie. 'space') does not occur anywhere in the pattern so the entire pattern is shifted to the right past the 'Δ'. The pattern 'T' is compared with the text string 'N'

7. 'N' does not occur anywhere in the pattern so the entire pattern is shifted to the right past the 'N'. The pattern 'T' is compared with the text string 'R'

8. 'R' occurs in the pattern which is accordingly shifted until the two 'R's are matched. The pattern 'T' is compared with the text string 'T' and the match extended left, one character at a time until the complete set of pattern characters has been matched successfully.

Thus, a total of only 14 character comparisons is required, despite the fact that N=43 and M=7.

The second algorithm was devised by Aho and Corasick (1975) and is based on the theory of finite state automata. A finite state automaton, or FSA, is a conceptual machine that can determine whether or not an input sequence matches a specified pattern; it is composed of five basic elements.

S - a set of states

R - a set of rules which determine the next state of the automaton given the current state and an input symbol

B - a beginning state from the set S

I - a set of input symbols acceptable to the automaton

F - a set of one (or more) final states from the set S

The operation of the FSA is simple. At the start it is in state B. Whenever a character arrives, the rules R are used to determine the next state of the FSA. This process continues until a final state is reached, indicating that a desired pattern has been matched. An important characteristic of an FSA is that it can be used to recognize one of many words input at the same time by speci-fying the proper transitions. This characteristic provides the basis for the use of FSAs in text searching systems since it provides a mechanism for the matching of the text string against *all* of a set of query patterns at the same time, thus making the cost of a search almost independent of the number of patterns once the FSA has been created.

Conversely, the other pattern matching algorithms described previously all allow only a single pattern to be matched against the text at any one time. In addition, the Aho-Corasick algorithm can be implemented so as to allow the searching of embedded substrings and of both fixed length and variable length don't care patterns, which cause problems for the Boyer-Moore algor-ithm. In practice, a pattern is specified by a state transition table containing the next state for the FSA and its output as a function of the current state and input character. By appropriate changes to the table, any desired pattern can be recognized. Thus, to use the FSA, some means must be found to create the state transition tables, and this is quite a complex procedure. Moreover, the tables are demanding of storage, and severe problems of efficiency can arise if the set of patterns is being constantly modified. When this is not the case, as for a set of queries that needs to be run again and again against new batches of text records as they are received, the algorithm provides an at-tractive retrieval mechanism. Aho and Corasick (1975) showed that their algorithm improved the speed of a library bibliographic search program by a factor of 5 to 10 when it was substituted in place of the simple pattern match-ing algorithm, the improvement in performance being more pronounced with larger numbers of patterns.

The great efficiency of the Aho-Corasick method has led to interest in hard-ware, rather than software, implementations of the algorithm. An example of this approach is described by Hollaar (1983); his group at the University of Utah have constructed a hardware text scanning device, analogous in purpose to the CAFS machine discussed in chapter 13, which contains a series of 'search engines'. Each search engine scans continuous text from its own large Winchester disk for the presence of query patterns, the actual pattern matching being effected by a VLSI implementation of a modified form of an FSA (Hsiao, 1983).

Text signatures

The algorithms described in the previous section achieve efficiencies in operation by reducing the number of characters in each document which need to be matched against the query patterns. The text signature approach to serial text scanning tries to eliminate some of the documents *in toto* from the pattern matching search.

A signature representation of a textual document, such as a journal article or a technical report, is a fixed-length bit string in which bits are set to describe the contents of the document. The bit string is created by applying some hashing-like[1] operation to each of the keywords or descriptors that characterise the document, the result of each such operation causing one or more bits in the string to be switched on (Harrison, 1971; Tharp and Tai, 1982). Once a file of signatures has been created, queries that are presented to the database may be searched using a two-stage retrieval mechanism. In the first stage, the query signature is compared with the set of document signatures. Matching operations upon strings of bits can generally be implemented very much more efficiently than can operations upon strings of characters, since the groups of bits comprising a computer word can be inspected in parallel, and thus this first-stage search is quick, despite the fact that all of the document signatures must be inspected in the search.

A detailed character matching procedure is then invoked for those documents that match at the signature level, and the computationally demanding second-stage search is restricted to small numbers of documents only. Such an approach can have a drastic effect on the execution time of a serial search. For example, Hickey (1979) reports an early experimental system, using a DEC-10 computer to scan 30 MB of data from the INSPEC database, in which serial scanning using the Aho-Corasick algorithm took more than 15 minutes elapsed time whereas most of the signature searches were completed within 45 to 90 seconds. Searches of 3.8 MB data from the Science Citation Index database were even quicker with some taking as little as 10 seconds.

The signatures are also very much smaller than the source documents from which they have been generated, and so, during a search, less data needs to be transferred into the processor from backing storage than would be the case if the entire file of full document texts had to be inspected. An individual re-

---

[1] Hashing : Using the digits or letters of a token to compute a value which, when suitably transformed, as by division, yields an address, or a bit position in a vector.

cord in a file of journal citations that contained the title and the abstract might well be some hundreds of words long, whereas the corresponding signature might be only a few hundreds of bits in length. This does, of course, assume that only relatively short documents are to be searched for in a database. If, instead, large full-text documents are to be stored, then the many words in a text will result in a signature in which the overwhelming majority of the bits are set. In such cases, the signature search cannot be expected to eliminate very much material prior to the pattern matching search. This problem can be overcome if full-text items are sub-divided into smaller units, each of which is allocated one signature. An appropriate choice of unit might be an individual paragraph or some fixed number of sentences. Such an arrangement requires that the retrieval software be able to identify the start and end of the of the group of signatures representing each of the documents in the signature file.

Another problem is that each bit in a signature denotes only the presence or absence of the text strings in a document which have been hashed to that location; it is therefore not possible to carry out proximity searches . . .

(INFORMATION (within three words of) RETRIEVAL)

. . . very efficiently since the relative positions of the two words can be identified only during the pattern matching search. Problems can also arise if weighting schemes, such as those described in the previous chapter, are used to indicate the relative degrees of importance of terms in queries and documents (Croft and Savino, 1988). Despite these limitations, the ease of updating and the speed of retrieval are attracting considerable interest, in particular for the implementation of text retrieval in office systems and multi-media information systems. (Christodoulakis and Faloutsos, 1984; Rabitti and Zizka, 1984). An operational example of a signature-based retrieval system is described by Dittmar et al. (1983) in the context of the CAS Online chemical substructure search system. Here, the signatures are bit strings denoting the presence or absence of specified fragment substructures in each of the molecules in the search file, rather than the presence or absence of text strings in documents. Only those structures for which a match is obtained at the bit string level undergo a second-stage, and computationally demanding, atom-by-atom isomorphism search to confirm the presence or absence of the query substructure.

Several methods are available for the creation of text signatures. In word-based methods, the document and query texts are scanned to eliminate commonly occurring words on a stop list and the remaining words, or word stems if a conflation procedure has been used, are processed by a conventional hashing algorithm which results in the conversion of the word's byte string into a location in the bit string which is set accordingly. The number of bits set in a signature will thus be equal to the number of non-common words in the document, or slightly less if, as can happen, two or more of these words hash to the same location.

Alternatively, each word can be used to set several bits using one of two approaches. The first adopts a word-based hashing function with the difference that each word is input to several different hashing functions with different divisors. The alternative substring-based methods involve breaking each word into its constituent n-grams, that is, fixed length substrings of length 'n' characters.

Figure 12.2 : Formation of a 'signature'

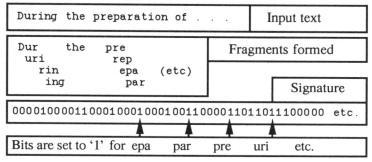

Each of these n-grams is then hashed to a location in the bit string, as is illustrated for the case of trigrams in figure 12.2.

Considerable care needs to be taken in deciding which signature generation method should be used. Substring-based methods are attractive since they allow the possibility of fuzzy word matching, that is, the retrieval of documents which have been indexed by terms that are slight variants of query terms, differing from them by only one or two n-grams. However, the use of substrings necessarily means that the occupancy of the bit string is likely to be quite high unless several signatures are used to characterise each document, in which case the storage requirement for the signature file is considerably greater.

The development of efficient and effective signature generation methods is an active area of research, as is the use of text signatures for best match, rather than Boolean, searching (Croft and Savino, 1988; Faloutsos, 1985).

13 Hardware for full text searching

Computers with conventional architectures have a number of fundamental limitations that make them inherently unsuitable for information retrieval applications (Hollaar, 1979; Shuegraf and Lea, 1983). Firstly, they can execute only a single instruction at a time, and each instruction operates on only one set of data at a time; additional loop control structures are required, therefore, if the same operation is to be applied to several data items, like comparing a character string against different sections of another string. Secondly, the arithmetic units are designed primarily for computational tasks rather than for text comparisons, which must be performed by treating the character strings as numbers. A further problem is the requirement that all data which is to be processed must be moved from high-capacity secondary or backing store into the main memory before the CPU can examine it. Not only are secondary storage devices slow in operation, but it is usually the case that the great bulk of the database is not relevant to a particular query.

Studies of large formatted data bases have indicated that nine times as much irrelevant data as relevant data must be brought into the main memory for processing, the so-called '90-10 rule' (Hsiao, 1980), and the hit rate for textual queries is usually very much less. Because of the difficulties inherent in using conventional computers for text retrieval, there is considerable interest in improving response times by the use of a range of computers that provide facilities for parallel processing. Some of these machines are discussed below.

Database machines

Database machines form a class of computer which has been developed specifically for the purposes of database scanning (Hollaar, 1979; Hsiao, 1980; Hsiao, 1983; Ozkarahan, 1986). Most of these machines provide content addressability by associating processing logic with the read/write heads of a disc unit to allow database searching and processing activities that would otherwise have been performed by the central processor of the host machine. Such devices circumvent the 90-10 rule since they pass only relevant data to the host machine, and the reduction in load on the central processor of the host frees it for other activities. Several small search processors are usually provided, each executing the same search and processing commands on different parts of the database, and this parallelism further reduces the time required for serial scanning.

Most database machines have been designed primarily to operate on formatted data and only as research prototypes (Salton and McGill, 1983; Hsiao, 1983). However, the ICL *Content Addressable Filestore,* or CAFS, is a commercial product available across the entire ICL[1] mainframe range which can be used for both data and text scanning. It consists of a cooperating group of special hardware units operating in conjunction with a conventional disk controller. While the latter continues to be responsible for normal file transfers in which data is either read or written in blocks, the CAFS units scan stored data in a continuous stream from disk, and pass back to the host only that small sub-set of the datastream that satisfies the query specified by the user (Carmichael, 1985; Haworth, 1985).

Incoming data from disk are scanned to locate points that are relevant for the direction of the search and retrieval activities such as the start of a page, a record or a relevant field. The datastream is passed through up to 16 key channels, operating independently and in parallel. Each key channel can hold one search criterion and compare it with the relevant fields of each data record. Masks can be used to exclude irrelevant bits or characters from comparison and each key channel can match up to 256 consecutive bytes within a record. When the end of a record has been detected, the information stored in the key channels is used to determine whether or not a record is a hit, using Boolean logic, quorum logic (i.e., 'M' matching words out of 'N'), or a combination of the two. The appropriate fields of hit records are then returned to the host after carrying out any necessary post-retrieval functions, like counting hit records, totalling specified fields, or finding maximum and minimum values.

For free text to be searchable in CAFS it must be encoded in a format consisting of an identifier byte, a length byte and then the actual string, for instance, an individual text word. The incorporation of the identifier and length bytes for each word in a variable length data element, such as a title or abstract, has the obvious disadvantage of increasing the storage space needed for the records, unless it is decided to store each word in a fixed length field, which again increases the storage requirement. The amount of data that needs to be scanned can be reduced by using a modified form of the signature approach discussed earlier in chapter 12. A bit map is created in which each word group is associated with a bit string specifying the presence or absence of that word in each fixed-length cell of the text store. This bit map is accessed to identify those cells which might satisfy the query and these are then scanned exhaustively as described above (Carmichael, 1984).

Early reports of the use of CAFS for text searching include papers by Kay (1985), who discusses the development of an office filing and retrieval system based on CAFS, and by Burnard (1985), who describes the use of CAFS at Oxford University Computing Services, including a 15 MB corpus of Shakespearean drama and the Bodleian Library pre-1920 catalogue. ICL has built CAFS into a number of quite diverse software products which span the range from conventional structured data systems to strongly text oriented products (figure 13.1). The original (circa 1979) 'brute force' approach to

---

[1] ICL is the information systems subsidiary of STC PLC.

searching unstructured text streams for target strings has been superseded by these later, and much more effective, forms.

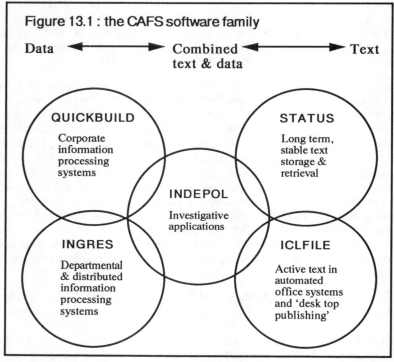

Figure 13.1 : the CAFS software family

Data ⟷ Combined text & data ⟷ Text

QUICKBUILD
Corporate information processing systems

STATUS
Long term, stable text storage & retrieval

INDEPOL
Investigative applications

INGRES
Departmental & distributed information processing systems

ICLFILE
Active text in automated office systems and 'desk top publishing'

The products shown in the left hand side of the diagram are essentially data oriented, with **QUICKBUILD** being applied mainly to the rapid development of analysis and reporting applications for corporate and strategic data, and with **INGRES** being a relational database suite used more for departmental data processing and reporting systems. CAFS is applied to the fast scanning of structured data, especially tables, and not only speeds up the searching process during retrievals, but reduces the need for index building and index storage space on the larger data sets.

On the right hand side of figure 13.1 are **STATUS** and **ICLFILE**, concerned with predominantly textual databases. Since STATUS incorporates its own specialised (and, in ICL implementations, optimised) indexing routines for full text, CAFS is not of particular value in dealing with retrievals from a stable database. It is used, however, to overcome the complementary problem that such indexing tends to be costly when done interactively. CAFS is applied to the unprocessed queue of new and modified documents so that these are immediately accessible to the user, and updating of the main database may be deferred to the much more efficient batch processors in the

STATUS Utility suite. In ICLFILE, on the other hand, documents in *revis-able* format (ODA or Office Document Architecture) are held on magnetic disc in a user friendly[1] 'file and folder' structure, and **profiles**, or short catalogue entries, of each document are placed in a CAFS file. The office user then has a simple form-filling way of quickly searching the profiles of a large document set through CAFS, while the original text body is kept in an appropriate form for re-use. Documents for long term retention may be transferred to STATUS as they move from office use to archive (Pavelin, 1987).

INDEPOL, which bridges the gap between data and text, was originally developed as a CAFS based storage and retrieval system for police and defence information systems - and in consequence has particularly strong and selective provisions for access security and for direct use by professional staff. It has subsequently been applied to credit assessment and fraud investigations, and to air safety inquiries. CAFS is used to treat data fields and text alike as access points for searching, and uses a simple, relational like dialogue or a form filling enquiry mode to make search formulation easy. There are no physical pointers between records, and associations are made by CAFS and the software without user intervention. New records, including those with text, may be quite informal, more like conversations than memos, or fully structured, and are *immediately* available for searching. It is a little surprising that this product has not been applied more widely - tasks such as Help Desk recording and analysis in large communications systems; software libraries at program and subroutine level; and the assessment of responses to public development proposals all show the same dual structure, and immediacy of application.

There are, of course, apart from these five packaged products, several ways in which programmers can access CAFS directly for specific applications. It is unlikely that either the diversity of potential application frameworks, or the technical need for such different expressions of the same hardware infrastructure were envisaged when CAFS was first proposed as a new concept around 1972, though the refusal to recognise any artificial distinction between text and data was certainly original. It will be of interest to see whether the later competing products follow the same development path.

Array processors

Parallelism in the CAFS system is manifested by the key channels and multiplexed datastream. A more extreme example of the use of parallel processing techniques for text retrieval is demonstrated by recent work on the class of parallel computers known as array processors or, less commonly, processor arrays. The important characteristic of an array processor is that it contains a large, two-dimensional (2-D) array of identical and very simple processing elements, or PEs. An individual PE consists of a single memory chip and a bit-serial arithmetic and logical unit which allows high level instructions,

---

[1]   The only use of this cliché in the whole book!

such as 32-bit addition, to be built up from cycles of basic one-bit instructions.

The basic design of an array processor allows all of the PEs to carry out the same operation in parallel. However, facilities are provided which allow some or many of the PEs to be disabled[1] during the course of a computation so that results are calculated for only some sub-set of the total number of PEs in the machine. Each PE is linked to its N, E, S and W neighbours and can read data from their stores. Moreover, row and column highways are provided to connect together sets of PEs in the 2-D array, allowing global operations to be carried out very effectively. The regular nature of the array and the simplicity of the individual PEs means that improvements in technology can be easily implemented without a radical restructuring of the basic architecture.

The control unit of an array processor carries out many of the functions of the control unit of a conventional computer in that it is responsible for the tasks of instruction fetch, decode and modify by registers. However, it does not generally *execute* instructions since most of the decoded instructions are sent, or broadcast, to the array of PEs; each PE then executes the instruction sequence on its own locally held data. An array processor is an example of the class of computers normally referred to as Single Instruction stream, Multiple Data stream (or SIMD), in which the same instruction is executed simultaneously by very large numbers of independent processors.

The two array processors considered here, the ICL *Distributed Array Processor*, or DAP, (Gostick, 1979) and the Thinking Machines Inc. *Connection Machine*, or CM, (Hillis, 1985) differ only slightly in their implementation of the basic array processor architecture. Current versions of the DAP have PE stores containing up to 1 Mbyte, as against only 4 Kbytes for the CM; however, the latter can have up to 256x256 PE arrays, as against a maximum of 64x64 for the DAP. In addition to nearest neighbour connections, the CM has a hypercube[2] network allowing packet-switched communication between arbitrary PEs.The bit-serial, word-parallel organisation of an array processor allows the same bit location to be inspected in all of the PEs simultaneously, making these machines very suitable for the processing of text signatures using both Boolean and best match operations; there have recently been two accounts published of best match signature scanning on array processors (Pogue and Willett, 1987; Stanfill and Kahle, 1986). Although the PEs in an array processor are connected in a 2-D array planar array, software allows them to be regarded as a linear array of PEs; thus a 64x64 DAP may be programmed as if it contained 4096 PEs. Each PE has sufficient memory for the storage of at least one text signature (for normal signature lengths) and it is thus possible to match a query signature against a set of 4096 document

---

[1]   disabled : computer jargon meaning 'turned off till further notice'

[2]   hypecube : a four dimensional analogue of the cube; here it represents the connexion pattern as the edges of its six constituent three dimensional cubes. (Don't panic!)

signatures in parallel. The location of each non-zero bit in the query signature is broadcast to the PEs. If the bit corresponding to this location is set in the document signature, a bit in common has been identified. The matches are noted and the process continued until all of the non-zero query bits have been processed in this way. A count is kept in each PE whenever a common bit is identified in that PE's signature. These counters are then sorted into decreasing order to allow the identification of the documents which are most similar to the query. With a small database, the local storage in the PEs may suffice to accommodate the complete set of document signatures. More generally, it may be necessary to replace the current set of signatures with another set from backing storage, so that the database is scanned in a series of blocks of documents, rather than just one document at a time as in a serial search on a conventional processor.

An operational example based on such an architecture has been described by Stanfill and Kahle (1986). Their experiments used some 16,000 articles from the Reuters wire service, a total of some 32 Mbytes of text, with a 128x128-PE CM hosted by a Symbolics 3600 Lisp machine where the full texts of the documents were stored on disc. Response times of about one second were reported, with much of this being accounted for by interface and support activities. The authors estimate execution times of between two and three minutes for searching of a 15 Gbytes database - given a sufficiently fast replacement scheme to swap new blocks of signatures into the PE stores.

Once the signature search has eliminated a large fraction of the file, the second, pattern matching search can be implemented on an array processor by storing one character from a document text in the same relative location in each PE. The characters in the query are then broadcast, one at a time, and compared with the character in each PE, so that the entire document text is inspected at the same time (assuming that the number of characters is less than the number of PEs in the processor). A flag is set in all PEs where the first query character occurs. The second query character is then broadcast and flags are again set where the character occurs; however, the flag in some PE is not set unless the flag in the preceding PE had been set as a result of the previous broadcast. Thus, using the query stem ALGORIT, flags would be set in response to the 'L' character only in those PEs which contained an 'L' **and** in which the PE to the left had a flag set to denote the presence of the initial 'A'.

This flagging procedure, which can be implemented very efficiently on an array processor using bit vectors, continues until all of the query characters have been broadcast. If there are any PEs flagged in response to the terminal query character, the query pattern is present in the document. The number of character comparisons required is thus of order $O(M)$ for a query pattern containing M characters. This description has been rather simplified for purposes of explanation and omits the need to load several documents into the processor, rather than just one, and the way in which this basic algorithm can be used to implement a range of don't care and proximity searches. Full details of the algorithm are presented in Carroll et al. (1988) who also report experiments that demonstrate the great efficiency of this procedure when compared with an implementation of the Aho-Corasick algorithm on a conventional minicomputer.

Transputer networks

An array processor is an example of a Single Instruction stream, Multiple Data stream, or SIMD, computer. They are so called since the same instruction is executed on locally stored data in all of the PEs at the same time (unless some of them have been previously disabled during the execution of the program). An alternative type of parallelism is exemplified by Multiple Instruction stream, Multiple Data stream, or MIMD, computers. Here, the parallelism arises from the fact that some, or many, processors can execute their own program simultaneously, while being able to communicate between themselves to meet the requirements of a particular application. Although originally developed to improve the performance of mainframes and supercomputers, MIMD systems are increasingly being based on networks of low cost, high performance microprocessors. An example of a series of microprocessors which has been designed specifically for parallel processing is the INMOS Transputer.

The availability of transputer networks seems to make serial text scanning a realistic prospect even on microcomputer systems, where the network could be use as a hardware accelerator to improve the performance of the basic host machine. Recent work has provided some evidence to support such a conclusion (Cringean et al., 1988). The study involved using networks of T414 transputers, linked together in a chain, with the transputer at one end of the chain acting as the interface between the network and the host machine. The T414 model transputer is a 10 MIPS[1], 32-bit RISC[2] processor with 2,000 bytes of on-chip memory, connections to off-chip memory and to backing storage, and four communication links which can be used to build up networks of transputers for highly parallel processing (Walker, 1985). The network is organised as a processor farm, or processor pool. Each processor runs the same program as the other members of the network, but on a different subset of the input data stream. The basic computational task which needs to be carried out by each processor is the matching of a set of query keyword stems against a document title and abstract. A query-document pair is distributed to the transputers in the pool as soon as there is a transputer available to process it, signalled by the receipt at the control transputer of a results message from the previous query-document pair. This is a highly

---

[1] MIPS : million instructions per second; a typical personal computer delivers about 1 MIP, but on a fairly rich instruction set.

[2] RISC : Reduced instruction set, containing only frequently used instructions.

efficient way of using a network for applications involving relatively little inter-processor communication relative to the computational load.

An important measure of an MIMD system is the relative speed-up which can be obtained, that is, the extent to which the scanning rate of the system varies with changes in the size of the network of processors. Ideally, the speed-up should be equal to the number of processors used so that a network containing five transputers would be able to scan text five times as fast as a single transputer. In practice factors such as communication and scheduling costs, or a limited amount of parallelism in the algorithm which is being executed, can lead to a sub-linear increase in the speed-up as more processors are added to the network. Commercial mainframe multiprocessors typically contain only a few processors because of this problem; one of the main claims made for the new generation of microprocessor-based multiprocessors is that they are less affected by it. Cringean et al. (1988) present speed-up figures obtained when the Boyer-Moore algorithm was used to search a set of 35 natural language queries and 1000 document titles and abstracts. The network contained between one and eleven transputers, with an additional transputer acting as the network controller and interface between the network and the host microcomputer. The maximum speed-up factor obtained with 11 transputers was 10.4 so that, although the gain is not quite linear, it does seem that transputer networks such as this can substantially increase the speed of text scanning in serial files. Further increases in performance were obtained when an initial signature match was used to reduce the pattern matching requirement.

There are some problems associated with this model. Only a very small set of documents was used and extension to larger files would probably incur substantial data communication costs owing to the need to transmit query-document pairs over the network to transputers as they become available. There are two ways in which this could be overcome. Firstly, a text compression algorithm can be used to reduce the amount of data which needs to be transmitted, effectively increasing the bandwidth of the data communications pathways within the network. An example of this is provided by the TEX-TRACT text scanner developed by Memex Information Engines, where text compression is used to allow an effective throughput of up to 2.5 times the speed of the standard storage interface in a DEC VAX VMS environment. Secondly, on-board memories containing up to 4 Mbytes are becoming available for use with transputers and thus a non-trivial amount of text can be stored immediately adjacent to the processor where it is to be scanned, so that only the queries need to be distributed over the network. Developments such as these suggest that transputers could provide a very effective means of microcomputer-based, serial text scanning.

The techniques described in the current and the previous chapter offer substantial increases in performance over a conventional serial search, especially when both the hardware and software approaches can be combined, as in the implementation of text signature searching on an array processor. Such systems are likely to become increasingly cost effective with the rapidly falling costs of parallel hardware of all sorts. Even with the advent of extensive parallelism in hardware, it is likely that the elapsed time for the completion of a serial scan of a large database will continue to exceed that of an inverted file search, and it has been suggested that even high-performance database machines may require the use of some sort of indexing strategy for large files of text (Hsiao, 1983).

This may be true but it should be remembered that the elapsed time, as perceived by the searcher, is the time taken to get a single retrieved document on to the screen of the terminal. Once this has been displayed, the user will be reading and determining whether it is useful while the actual search is continuing, and hit records are being stored for subsequent inspection as the search progresses. In an inverted file search, conversely, no records at all are available for inspection until all of the inverted file list operations have been completed. Thus an acceptable response time *is* achievable in a serial scan so long as the query is able to produce at least one appropriate document within the first few seconds of the search. Given such a strategy, we believe that there is a future for large text retrieval systems based on serial scanning.

14 What to look for in a system

As it stated in the Introduction - *'There are, being realistic, some bounds to the total information system argument! Total informations systems are not going to be used for real time control; or for high volume transaction pro - cessing (except maybe in special 'read only' contexts); or for purely numeric computing such as matrix processing'.* Of course, a specialised routine for transaction processing or for real time interactions *might* be invoked through a text system 'window' - which sounds unlikely but is not too remote from some of the more imaginative applications which have been reported - like storing and retrieving data from high energy physics experiments at Culham Laboratories, or producing North Sea Oil and Gas Production statistics (Ashford and Matkin, 1982).

Accepting a reasonable boundary, what should a prospective user of a total information product reasonably expect to find when it is unwrapped and installed? In this chapter we consider software and its vendors; differences in dealing with hardware based solutions; and the special case of micro computer based products. The functional and performance criteria are described as **necessary** or **must** or **required** (that is, if absent, it is not really a total information management system at all); **desirable** (needed to be realistically competitive); and **options** which are interesting but non-essential. The research and development topics covered in chapters 10 and 11, such as 'intelligent front ends' should be regarded as likely to become 'desirable' for many users by 1992.

All of the usual rules for appraisal of a software supplier apply to text-based products. It is reasonable to expect financial stability, development plans, full documentation, well-defined maintenance and upgrade services, training programmes, 'help' desks, on-site support in times of crisis, and a vendor independent, lively user group. The last is sometimes very productive, as most vendors are ready to admit that users do things with their products that the designers had never envisaged, and it is at the user group meetings that many of the bright ideas get passed on.

A few consultancy firms have developed special expertise in design and support services in this field, some for particular applications like litigation support. It is, however, not common to find the necessary combination of *information* skills, for analysing the user's requirements and the vocabulary control, classification or linguistic aspects, and also the *computing* knowledge of database practice and operating systems required for confidence in undertaking large implementations. Prospective clients do well to check the *individual* skills and experience of the staff they are offered on consultancy assignments (Gurnsey & White, 1988b).

In dealing with relational DBMS + text implementations, *Codd's Rules* are, if sensibly applied, a useful basis for systematic assessment of the R.DBMS part. Based on the relational algebra which is the theoretical foundation for relational database design, these rules deal with :

- Data representation in tables;

- Access paths and conventions;

- Consistency of presentation both of the data itself and of database directories and such aids as a data dictionary;

- 'High level' and uniform treatment of retrieval, insertion, modification and removal of data;

- Data independence of hardware or storage decisions;

. . . . and a number of more technical considerations.

Detailed consideration falls outside the scope of the present book, but for those interested in appraisal of any particular R.DBMS + Text product, a concise recent statement will be found in Codd (1987). Otherwise consult Date (1986), Chapter 15. There is, unfortunately, no way of being so explicit and precise in defining formal criteria for text systems!

Scope of the text processor

Dealing efficiently and comprehensively with the text part of a document management system is the fundamental requirement, since not only does text represent a major component of most documents, the text part is technically more awkward than the data management structures.

Because of the large volumes and unpredictable structures of text documents, systems must not impose restrictions on database size or layout other than those arising from hardware limitations. Long texts, or if appropriate, chapters of documents, should be held as individual records, and must be indexable either in their entirety, or optionally, over designated sections only. Both free format text, and text with superimposed structures must be accommodated, and a provision is needed for fields such as dates, numeric values, strings of special characters, which allow data validation, range comparisons, sorting and string searching. There must be no arbitrary constraint on the content or form of natural language text.

When the text is indexed, the system must be able to set aside common or stop words to avoid cluttering the index with terms of little retrieval value. It is often useful also to be able to specify that only go or pass words (from a thesaurus or data dictionary[1]) should be indexed at all. Phrases from keyword sections may similarly be usefully matched to a control list, especially in library and document management applications. At the present stage of development, Boolean query formulation using terms from the document set appears to be indispensable - the promising alternatives of term weighting or relevance ranking have not yet graduated from the laboratory into stable, large volume production tools, and some employ an intermediate Boolean search formulation anyway. When full text of documents is stored, indexing at word level is highly desirable, to enable queries on phrases and closely located terms to be performed directly, rather than by sequential string searching on the large volumes of text which tend to be retrieved at intermediate stages - and the longer the working units of text, the more tedious the string search becomes sing conventional hardware, and especially on PC family computers.

During search dialogues, and especially prior to display of intermediate or final results, it is necessary for the user to be kept informed of the number of items in the current retrieved set. Combination of previously 'saved' sets of results is often found useful[2], but the ability to go back one step when a search refinement results in an *empty* retrieved list is really important! Because so many of the search processes are naturally interactive, it is desirable to provide an on-line editor also - often the system editor is suitable. However, the bulk input of new text, and the periodic output of selected material for reports and reprocessing, makes efficient batch processes necessary. Sorting of search results, and editing for final presentation are common and desirable requirements.

Right truncation, or removal of selected characters from the right hand end of a search term, is necessary in European languages at least, to deal with plurals and other inflected endings. Left-hand truncation, and stemming, which truncates based on syntactic divisions within words, have specialised applications, for example to chemical name searching and in agglutinative languages (Finnish, Turkish, some Semitic, and some Indic languages), but seem to be optional in other cases. What is, however, often found to be valuable, is to have a window of some sort (or a 'frequency' command) giving access to the terms and their number of occurrences in the inverted file. This is of use in planning large searches, and in sorting out why an apparently reasonable search finds no relevant documents.

Ideographic languages (Chinese, Korean, some aspects of Japanese) have their own suite of problems and opportunities. Stemming is unhelpful, as characters are seen as a whole. On the other hand, some way of binding two

---

[1]   data dictionary : the directory, or sometimes separate subsystem, where a DBMS maintains details of fields, tables, and security requirements, and so a convenient place to store lists of preferred or allowable text values for use by the parser (chapter 4).

[2]   sets : may be highly (even emotionally) rated by those whose first or only contact with text retrieval was made on the on-line data vendor systems. It is a reasonable feature when sensibly applied to limit the user to small teleprocessing transactions.

or more characters into a concept is desirable, and in library practice at least, the use of subject indexes in controlled language to assure reasonably complete retrievals appears to be general practice (eg using the Pin Ying transliteration, 'America' = two linked characters **Mei_guó; mei** alone is 'pretty' and **guó** is 'place'; **diàn** = 'electricity', but **diàn_shì** means 'television'). Since there are many meanings for some characters, and several for many, context is important in presentation, and stop words have little application. On the other hand, if the two-byte representation of characters is used, a given Chinese text takes up less storage space on disc than its English equivalent, sometimes by as much as one-fifth. At the time of writing, (mid-1988), the vendors of STATUS and TRIP had announced English / Chinese dual versions, and a Chinese version of the UNISYS UNIDAS package has been locally adapted in Beijing (Lin, 1988 - a useful review; Zeng, 1987).

Reverting to English and similar languages, synonyms are required for the common case where a concept occurs in several equivalent or near equivalent forms (DEC = Digital Equipment Corporation; sulphur = sulfur etc.). If the subject of a database requires control of its indexing language, because of technical complexity or rate of change of concepts, (or, maybe, in some cases, the preconceptions of information specialists), then a synonym feature may be extended into a thesaurus, or hierarchic grouping of terms and phrases by meaning, rather than merely syntactic value. Limit functions to warn users who have launched costly searches and offer a chance to break off and reformulate a query have been found valuable and reassuring where they are implemented[1].

In the display of results, as well as ways to route text to system files, a facility to browse forward and backward in the text database itself and in retrieved subsets is required. Display of all or part of a retrieved text is necessary, and for full text applications, an option to display the 'context' of specified terms in a document, or to 'zoom' to such terms in a long text must be provided. Sequential search for target strings (scanning), with wild card options is needed, if only to deal with text containing embedded 'unknown's, or special characters excluded by the rules of the parser.

In R.DBMS + Text systems the option to use either 'fixed' or 'long text' domain types (or both) has many applications, and is probably necessary. It is desirable for all of the system files (inverse file, pointers, retrieved list etc.) to be kept as standard tables, as many program embedded applications can take advantage of access to this information directly. This may also substitute for the 'frequency' or 'window on the inverse file' requirements. Simple commands (or macros) to format results tables are desirable. However it is achieved, *some sort* of provision for customising users' needs at the front end interface is necessary, as often the information itself in the retrieval proc-

---

[1] Limit functions also save trouble with unobserved visitors to exhibition stands where on-line demonstrations are running!

ess is difficult enough, without making the work station appear unnecessarily hostile.

Performance

Text systems notoriously consume computer resources. There are several ways of achieving good system performance, and the best products are at least ten times as fast in text acquisition, three times as fast in retrieval, and one half as space demanding as those among the weakest which are still commercially available. What is necessary for a total information product is that the vendor has taken performance seriously, and adopted one of the viable strategies to ensure that computer resources are not unnecessarily dissipated. Not all of the possible ways of performance improvement can be applied at once, and the best trade-off requires some judgement by the designer. The following paragraphs summarize the main issues involved.

Separation of the inverse file, the pointer list and the text itself affects performance in two ways. During updates, the processing of each file may be adjusted to its structure, and bulk runs can be subdivided into parsing, sorting, deletion of index terms, inserting new entries, to reduce run times and provide restart points. An addition of 20Mb of new text which results in the use of 6 hours elapsed time to update an existing 100Mb database on a lightly loaded minicomputer is not exceptional - so restart points and process statistics are highly desirable. The option of incremental updating versus periodic concatenation of databases was discussed in chapter 5.

In interactive working, the majority of search processes should be performed on the inverse file and the pointer list - fixed format, fast to access - leaving the much slower variable length text file until the display stage, when the user has the initial results on screen to think about anyway. Compression of the text file, originally seen as conserving disc space, turns out to have access time advantages as fewer blocks need to be read - but it involves an overhead of packing and unpacking. On a large database, using magnetic disc storage, or even on quite a small one on CD-ROM optical disc, the effect of putting the major files in the best place - which may mean on separate disc drives - can be a dramatic improvement in retrieval times. It does, however, usually need operating system skills to get it right, and the vendor should be prepared to help.

All other gains may be cast away if volume text must be keyboarded from original papers. A suite of ancillary programs to accept OCR files; to download the contents of other text databases; to reformat word processor texts; and to interpret typesetter tapes is very important. Soon it will be reasonable to ask for automatic selection of keywords or phrases from a thesaurus, automatic clustering of like documents to speed retrieval and aid browsing, and maybe entry of text from audio sources. One INFO-DB+ user in North America, with a large (over 1,000 Mb) text database, has added a small cluster of

MicroVAX processors as a special purpose 'back-end' to a large DEC VAX minicomputer. This MicroVAX 'farm' holds, in solid state memory, rather than on disc, a thesaurus to aid classification and subsequent searching, and could potentially be used in scanning and subject clustering of incoming texts[1]. This may represent a useful future option for large, full text database systems, where the scale and performance requirements justify the investment in extra hardware and software complexity.

Mark-up tolerance

Especially in dealing with the text from office automation systems, but whenever the data in storage is both revisable and derived from word processors or desk top publishing work stations, provision is desirable for dealing with the special codes used for manipulating text in its presentation format. Three main approaches seem to be practical. The first is to store the text body twice, once in fully marked up revisable format, and again in a compact and more easily handled internal version; the latter is indexed and shown on screen (BASIS with DEC All-in-1; STATUS with DG CEO and with IBM PROFS; INFO-DB+ with WPS+, MASS11, WORDMARK, etc). This causes increased space overheads, but is reliable, performs well in interactive searching, and limits programming and maintenance costs.

The second method proceeds as the first, but discards the internal format text after indexing, so that the display stage refers to the fully marked up text in its word processor format. Space is saved, and presentation improved, at the expense of some delay in accessing multiple text files, and a wider opportunity for difficulties to occur in recovery from transient hardware faults.

The third approach is to retain mark-up in the text file, but use a reserved character to enclose and make invisible the word processor special codes (BASIS and BRS/SEARCH with WPS+, DISSOS etc.; DM, ORACLE*Text; STATUS on WANG). This is, in principle, more efficient, but is less common so far in practice, and each product requires a steadily increasing repertoire of decoding and interpretation tables as the word processors evolve.

Hybrid systems

There are probably around 100 text retrieval packages on the market for mainframes and minicomputers, and 150 for micro computers, including some overlap. Each year twenty new names appear, and about as many are 'no longer marketed'. Of all the 'live' systems, fewer than twenty can be regarded as *total* information management products, and the feature most often missing is the ability to interact on a practical level with software to handle numeric data, vector graphics, digitised images and similar 'non-text' but common and essential information carriers.

---

[1] Henry T Cochran, at a Henco Seminar, July 1988.

The required features are some form of macro or command language to 'hide' the inner processes from the user; a gateway to the operating system; one or more application dedicated handlers; and support from the package vendor to the user's systems programmers. When digitised images are involved, interfaces to compression / decompression servers for bit streams, and high capacity communications channels are likely to be necessary, and in most cases good quality graphics screens compatible with the normal text based input / output.

It is also necessary to provide adequate recovery features to restore a standard *user* state when a system fault occurs between applications, as an operating system prompt is less than friendly to the non-programmer!

Portability

Real life information systems often have much longer lives than the equipment on which they run, and large systems may be split over several minicomputers, or have segments down loaded[1] on to micro computers for local use. It is, perhaps, idealistic to hope that the version of a package would be *identical* from one make of machine to another. Some come very close, limited mainly by the need to write a minority of the program code in assembly language to deal efficiently with input / output and a few critical process routines. Compatibility of file structures between different manufacturers' equipment is also desirable, to make the best of mixed installations, and to give flexibility in migration to new suppliers; it is not, unfortunately, too common. The ability to build prototype applications at low cost on a micro computer, maybe even buying copies of two or more packages to try out at this low cost level, and then migrating to a minicomputer or mainframe with minimum readjustment has been found to be of great value in projects involving flexible or innovative requirements.

All aspects of portability would be rated as highly desirable.

Hardware-based text retrievers

The majority of the hardware-based systems currently available are directed towards straight-forward, large scale document retrieval, and few moves towards integration of graphics or images have been reported. If such systems as CAFS, NEBSYS, Gould MEMEX or the Britten-Lee systems do develop a total information capability, then the criteria set out here should generally apply. Those products which use document signatures (chapter 12) for a first pass search tend to slow down abruptly on phrase and word co-location handling unless special arrangements are made to speed up the string

---

[1] down loading : the process of copying data, text or software from a host machine to a local, usually micro computer system, having - of course - negotiated permission to do so and paid appropriate copyright or licence fees when required.

searches within the text partitions to which the signatures refer. The use of transputer clusters for this purpose may soon be important (chapter 13).

Total information on micros

Small scale document retrieval systems have been successfully delivered on the larger micro computers. They are subject to the limitations of MS-DOS and similar operating systems, but can usefully deal with up to twenty million characters of original text on a hard disc. Several can access CD-ROM and WORM text files, and a few have been reported linked to image systems. UNIX versions are often larger, and offer limited multi-user capability. Portability and prototyping were dealt with above.

What the prospective user needs to check is :

- that the system can deal with the acquisition and indexing of the required volumes of text in a reasonable time - some micros are slow;

- that a single user system is enough for the planned applications, or that the multi-user facility promised by the vendor actually works at a reasonable pace when the full database is installed;

- on CD-ROM systems, that the scope of the retrieval software is adequate for the user's needs - some are very slow, and limited in the facilities they offer;

- on magnetic disc systems, that back-up routines are available, easy to use, and foolproof. Copying the back-up version on top of the current is not too difficult under MS-DOS, and it hurts!

Otherwise, it is important to remember that smaller scale and lower prices do not necessarily lead to less complexity, and that the expenditure on people will generally far outweigh all other costs on a micro computer-based project.

The following Figures 14.1 and 14.2 summarize the criteria involved in choosing the best system for a given application. If several databases are required, then the best software is likely to be that which satisfies the most complex task, and the others will then use simpler sub-sets of the overall system.

Figure 14.1 : Criteria for selection - mainly text based information

The selection of a database model and software for information retrieval depends, as shown in the figures, on the nature of the data, the scale of the application, and the form in which retrieved results are to be presented.

If the database contains predominantly text information, or text plus images, then figure 14.1 is appropriate, as access will be based principally on the content of the records. If on the other hand numeric or coded data is more important, use figure 14.2, since access will be by the structure rather than the content of the data directly.

The five categories of delivery system for the information from the database are shown down the left hand column of each figure. They subdivide by the form of delivery - on-line where the retrieval produces the whole answer; and indirect, where there is a second stage in the retrieval. Further categories depend on whether the text is revisable (in word processors etc.) or not; and on how the indirect sources are stored and handled.

For KEY see figure 14.2

Text based information systems

Access path — Form of delivery	Access based on content of records			
Subdivided by form of delivery - - - - and content ==>	Text body itself		Added keywords	
	Text only	Text + image or graphics	Text only	Text + image or graphics
Delivery on-line : RFT - small scale, up to, say, 20Mb	(hatched)	(hatched)	File + folder model	File + folder + TRF
Delivery on-line : RFT - large scale	Free text (FTX) + TRF	Free text (FTX) + TRF(s)	Free text or R.DBMS + TRF	Free text or R.DBMS + TRF(s)
Delivery on-line : FFT - final form of text, which may include numbers	Free text (FTX) is ideal	FTX or ITX + TRF hybrids	FTX or R.DBMS	ITX or R.DBMS + TRF(s)
Delivery indirect : Storage on paper or analogues of paper	ITX + physical delivery	ITX + physical delivery	ITX + physical delivery	ITX + physical delivery
Delivery indirect : Storage on computer media	ITX + TRF	ITX + TRF(s)	ITX + TRF	ITX + TRF(s)

Figure 14.2 : Criteria for selection - mainly numeric information

Key to terms used :

Numeric & coded data information systems

Form of delivery	Access based on structure of records			
	Linear structures		Nets & hierarchies	
	Text only	Text + image or graphics	Text only	Text + image or graphics
Subdivided by form of delivery - - - - and content ==>				
Delivery on-line : RFT - small scale, up to , say, 20Mb	ISAM + TRF	ISAM + TRF	R.DBMS (mostly)	R.DBMS + TRF
Delivery on-line : RFT - large scale	/////	/////	R.DBMS + TRF	R.DBMS + TRF(s)
Delivery on-line : FFT - final form of text, which may include numbers	ISAM	ISAM + TRF	R.DBMS > DBMS	R.DBMS + TRF
Delivery indirect : Storage on paper or analogues of paper	/////	/////	R.DBMS + physical transfer	R.DBMS + physical transfer
Delivery indirect : Storage on computer media	Facsimile or similar simple TRF	Facsimile or similar simple TRF	R.DBMS + TRF	R.DBMS + TRF(s)

Access path

FTX : full text retrieval, based on inverse file indexing of terms taken from the actual body of text

ITX : indicative text retrieval, using added keywords or profiles, but the same sort of inverse file indexes

DBMS : conventional structured database management system - and R.DBMS : relational DBMS, a few with inverse file text retrieval also

ISAM : indexed sequential access

TRF : transfer of a file of an inherently different structure - and TRF(s) : multiple transfers of different file structures

RFT : revisable form of text, eg by a word processing or typesetting software package

FFT : text in final form, no longer 'marked up' for word processor or typesetter manipulation

Mb : megabytes (million characters) of data, nett, before storage and indexing overheads (as used here)

110

15 Sources of further information

Directories

Text Retrieval : a directory of software, edited by Robert Kimberley. 2nd Edition (Gower, Aldershot, and Brookfield, Vt.). This is a detailed loose-leaf guide to over 100 products and is kept reasonably up to date. There are also many short references in the standard EDP industry directories.

Periodicals

The literature is somewhat scattered, but good sources outside the computer science journals are :

Annual Review of Information Science and Technology (Elsevier); Information Media & Technology (Cimtech, Hatfield); Information Processing & Management (Pergamon); Journal of the American Society for Information Science (Wiley); Journal of Documentation (Aslib, London); Journal of Information Science (North-Holland); Online Review (Learned Information, Oxford); Program (Aslib).

For on-line searches, start with IFI/Plenum Information Science Abstracts; INSPEC Computer and Control Abstracts and IT Focus; and the Library Association LISA.

Conferences and seminars run by the *Institute of Information Scientists,* and the *British Computer Society - Information Retrieval Specialist Group* are also usually valuable. The latter group also run an annual Research Colloquium which is of value in exposing new ideas and concepts. There are joint ACM/BCS and ACM/SIGIR conferences for those who can afford the time and money.

Most of the major commercial package vendors have user groups, and several run worth while, if specialised meetings. They also produce newsletters, which may be useful.

Exhibitions

In the United Kingdom the most interesting events are probably *Information Showcase* (March); *Online Information* (December) - the exhibition rather than the meeting; *Optical Information Systems* (May)

References

AGARD, (1986) *The application of microcomputers to aerospace and defence scientific and technical information work.* AGARD Lecture Series no. LS149. Neuilly sur Seine : AGARD.

Aho, A.V. and Corasick, M.J. (1975) Efficient string matching : an aid to bibliographic search. Communications of the ACM vol. 18 pp. 333-340.

Aitchison, J., and Gilchrist A. (1988) *Thesaurus construction : a practical manual.* 2nd edition. London : Aslib.

Ashford, J.H., and Matkin, D.I. (1982) A review of the applications of STATUS in July 1982. (in) *Information technology in 1982.* (LA Conference Proceedings Series in Library Automation) London : The Library Association.

Ashford, J.H. and Scott, C.M. (1978) *ADLIB, an adaptive management system for special libraries.* Maidenhead : Lipman Management Resources Limited

Ashford, J.H., (1987a) Information structures for office automation (in) *Information handling for the office - full text rules OA?* London : Taylor Graham.

Ashford, J.H., (1987b) Text storage and retrieval in the ORACLE relational database system. Program vol. 21, pp. 108-123.

Boyer, R.S. and Moore, J.S. (1977) A fast string searching algorithm. Communications of the ACM vol. 20 pp. 762-772.

Brookes, B.C. (1984) The Haitun dichotomy and the relevance of Bradford's Law. Journal of Information Science vol. 8, pp. 19-24.

Carmichael, J.W.S. (1984) The application of ICL's Content Addressable Filestore to text storage and retrieval. Miller, J.H.H. (*ed.*) *PROTEXT I: Proceedings of the First International Conference on Text Processing.* Dublin: Boole Press, pp. 3-11.

Carmichael, J.W.S. (1985) History of the ICL Content-Addressable Filestore (CAFS). ICL Technical Journal vol. 4 pp. 352-357.

Carroll, D.M., Pogue, C.A. and Willett, P. (1988) Bibliographic pattern matching using the ICL Distributed Array Processor. Journal of the American Society for Information Science (in press).

Cercone, N. and McCalla, G. (1986) Accessing knowledge through natural language. Advances in Computers vol. 25, pp. 1-99.

Choueka, Y., Fraenkel, A. S., and Klein, S. T. (1988) Compression of concordances in full-text retrieval systems. (in) Y. Chiaramella (*ed*) *11th International Conference on Research & Development in Information Retrieval, Grenoble, June 1988.* (ACM / SIGIR) Grenoble : Presses Universitaires de Grenoble.

Christodoulakis, S. and Faloutsos, C. (1984) Design considerations for a message file server. IEEE Transactions on Software Engineering SE-10 pp. 201-210.

Cleverdon, C. (1984) Optimizing convenient online access to bibliographic databases. Information Services and Use vol. 4, pp. 37-47.

Coates, E., Lloyd, G. and Simandl, D. (1978) *BSO, Broad System of Ordering, Schedule and Index.* FID Publication No. 564. The Hague: International Federation for Documentation.

Codd, E. F. (1987) Codd's 12 rules for relational DBMS. The Relational Journal, Issue 1.

Cringean, J.K., Manson, G.A., Willett, P. and Wilson, G.A. (1988) Efficiency of text scanning in bibliographic databases using microprocessor-based multiprocessor networks. Journal of Information Science *(in press).*

Croft, W.B. and Harper, D.J. (1979) Using probabilistic models of document retrieval without relevance information. Journal of Documentation vol. 35, pp. 285-295.

Croft, W.B. and Savino, P. (1988) Implementing ranking strategies using text signatures. ACM Transactions on Office Information Systems vol. 6 pp. 42-62.

Croft, W.B. and Thompson, R. (1987) I^{3}R: a new approach to the design of document retrieval systems. Journal of the American Society for Information Science vol. 38, pp. 389-404.

Davies, R. (Editor) (1986). *Intelligent information systems : progress and prospects.* Chichester: Ellis Horwood.

Dittmar, P.G., Farmer, N.A., Fisanick, W., Haines, R.C. and Mockus, J. (1983) The CAS Online search system. I. General design and selection, generation and use of search screens. Journal of Chemical Information and Computer Sciences vol. 23 pp. 93-102.

Faloutsos, C. (1985) Access methods for text. Computing Surveys vol. 17 pp. 49-74.

Freund, G.E. and Willett, P. (1982) Online identification of word variants and arbitrary truncation searching using a string similarity measure. Information Technology: Research and Development vol. 1 pp. 177-187.

Fries, J., and Brown, J. (1987) Business information on CD-ROM : the Datext service at Dartmouth College, New Hampshire. Program vol. 21, pp. 1-12.

Gilreath, C. L. (1984) *Computerized literature searching : research strategies and databases.* Boulder CO and London : Westview Press.

Gostick, R.W. (1979) Software and algorithms for the Distributed Array Processors. ICL Technical Journal 2 116-135.

Gurnsey, J. and White, M. (1988a) Electronic publishing : a reprise. Information Media and Technology vol. 21, pp. 170-173.

Gurnsey, J. and White, M. (1988b) *Information consultancy.* London : Bingley.

Hall, J. L. (1986) *Online bibliographic databases.* London : Aslib.

Harrison, M. (1971) Implementation of the sub-string test by hashing. Communications of the ACM vol. 14 pp. 777-779.

Harter, S.P. (1978) Statistical approaches to automatic indexing. Drexel Library Quarterly, vol. 14, pp. 57-74.

Haworth, G.M. (1985) The CAFS System today and tomorrow. ICL Technical Journal vol. 4 pp. 365-392.

Hendley, A. H. (1985) *Videodiscs, compact discs and optical discs.* (Cimtech publication no. 23) Hatfield, Herts. : Cimtech.

Hendry, I.G., Willett, P. and Wood, F.E. (1986a) INSTRUCT : a teaching package for experimental methods in information retrieval. Part 1. The users' view. Program vol. 20, pp. 245-263.

Hendry, I.G., Willett, P. and Wood, F.E. (1986b) INSTRUCT : a teaching package for experimental methods in information retrieval. Part 2. Computational aspects. Program vol. 20, pp. 382-393.

Hickey, T. (1979) Searching linear files on-line. Online Review vol. 1 pp. 53-58.

Hillis, D. (1985) *The Connection Machine.* Cambridge, MA : MIT Press.

Hollaar, L.A. (1979) Unconventional computer architectures for information retrieval. Annual Review of Information Science and Technology vol. 14 pp. 129-151.

Hollaar, L.A. (1983) The Utah text retrieval project. Information Technology: Research and Development vol. 2, pp. 155-168.

Horspool, R.N. (1980) Practical fast matching in strings. Software - Practice and Experience vol. 10 pp. 501-506.

Hsiao, D.K. (1980) Data base computers. Advances in Computers vol. 19 pp. 1-64.

Hsiao, D.K. (1983) *Advanced database machine architecture.* Englewood Cliffs, NJ: Prentice-Hall.

Kay, M.H. (1985) Textmaster - a document retrieval system using CAFS-ISP. ICL Technical Journal vol. 4 pp. 455-467.

Keyhoe, C.A. (1985) Interfaces and expert systems for online retrieval. Online Review vol. 9, pp. 489-505.

Kimberley, R., *ed.* (1988) *Text retrieval : a directory of software,* edited by Robert Kimberley. 2nd Edition. Aldershot, and Brookfield, Vt. : Gower. (Loose leaf index, updated reasonably frequently.)

King, M. *ed.* (1983) *Parsing natural language.* London : Academic Press.

Knuth, D.E., Morris, J.H. and Pratt, V.R. (1977) Fast pattern matching in strings. SIAM Journal of Computing vol. 6 pp. 323-350.

Kracsony, P., Kowalski, G. and Meltzer, A. (1981) Comparative analysis of hardware versus software text search. Oddy, P.N., Robertson, S.E., van Rijsbergen, C.J. and Williams, P.W. (editors) *Information Retrieval Research* London: Butterworth, pp. 268-279.

Lennon, M., Peirce, D.S., Tarry, B.D. and Willett, P. (1981) An evaluation of some conflation algorithms for information retrieval. Journal of Information Science, vol. 3, pp. 177-183.

Lin, S.C. (1988) Development of computer applications in Chinese information centres. Journal of Information Science vol. 14, pp.195-203.

Lovecy, I. (1984) *Automating library procedures : a survivor's handbook.* London : The Library Association.

Marcus, R.S. (1983) An experimental comparison of the effectiveness of computers and humans as search intermediaries. Journal of the American Society for Information Science vol. 34, pp. 381-404.

Noreault, T., Koll, M. and McGill, M.J. (1977) Automatic ranked output from Boolean searches in SIRE. Journal of the American Society for Information Science vol. 28, pp. 333-339.

Oxborrow, E.A. (1986) *Databases and database systems : concepts and issues.* Bromley : Charwell Bratt Ltd.; Lund, Sweden : Studentlitteratur.

Ozkarahan, E. (1986) *Database machines and database management.* Englewood Cliffs, NJ: Prentice-Hall.

Pavelin, J.E. (1987) ICLFILE - office document filing system (in) *Information handling for the office - full text rules OA?* London : Taylor Graham.

Perry, S.A. and Willett, P. (1983) A review of the use of inverted files for best match searching in information retrieval systems. Journal of Information Science, vol. 6, pp. 59-66.

Pogue, C.A. and Willett, P. (1987) Use of text signatures for document retrieval in a highly parallel environment. Parallel Computing vol. 4, pp. 259-268.

Pollitt, A.S. (1984) A 'front-end' system: an expert system as an online search intermediary. Aslib Proceedings vol. 36, pp. 229-234.

Porter, M.F. (1980), An algorithm for suffix stripping. Program, vol. 14, pp. 130-137.

Prowse, S. G. (1986) Use of BRS/SEARCH in OPAC experiments. Program vol. 20, pp. 178-195.

Rabitti, F. and Zizka, J. (1984) Evaluation of access methods to text documents in office systems. van Rijsbergen, C.J. (*ed.*) *Research and Development in Information Retrieval* Cambridge: Cambridge University Press, pp 21-40.

van Rijsbergen, C.J. (1979) *Information retrieval.* London: Butterworth.

Robertson, S.E. (1974) Specificity and weighted retrieval. Journal of Documentation vol. 30, pp. 41-46.

Robertson, S.E. (1986) On relevance weight estimation and query expansion. Journal of Documentation vol. 42, pp. 182-188.

Robertson, S.E. and Sparck Jones, K. (1976) Relevance weighting of search terms. Journal of the American Society for Information Science vol. 27, pp. 129-146.

Robertson, S.E., Thompson, C.L., Macaskill, M.J. and Bovey, J.D. (1986) Weighting, ranking and relevance feedback in a front-end system. Journal of Information Science vol. 12, pp. 71-75.

Salton, G. (1986) Recent trends in automatic information retrieval. *Proceedings of the Ninth International Conference on Research and Development in Information Retrieval,* pp. 1-10.

Salton, G., Fox, E.A. and Wu, H. (1983) Extended Boolean information retrieval. Communications of the ACM vol. 26, pp. 1022-1036.

Salton, G. and McGill, M.J. (1983) *Introduction to modern information retrieval.* New York: McGraw-Hill.

Schuegraf, E.J. and Lea, R.M. (1983) A proposal for an associative file store with run-time indexing. Part 1: System Descriptors. Information Technology : Research and Development vol. 2 pp. 73-88.

Smit, G.D.V. (1982) A comparison of three string matching algorithms. Software - Practice and Experience vol. 12, pp. 57-66.

Smith, L.C. (1987) Artificial intelligence and information retrieval. Annual Review of Information Science and technology vol. 22, pp. 41-77.

Sparck Jones, K. (1972) A statistical interpretation of term specificity and its application in retrieval. Journal of Documentation vol. 28, pp. 11-21.

Sparck Jones, K. and Tait, J.I. (1984) Automatic search term variant generation. Journal of Documentation vol. 40, pp. 50-66.

Stanfill, C. and Kahle, B. (1986) Parallel free-text search on the Connection Machine system. Communications of the ACM vol. 29 pp. 1229-1239.

Staud, J. L. (1988) The universe of online databases : reality and model(s). Journal of Information Science vol. 14, pp. 141-158.

Stibic, V. (1980) Influence of unlimited ranking on practical online search strategy. Online Review vol. 4, pp. 273-278.

Tedd. L. A. (1984) *An introduction to computer-based library systems.* 2nd Edition. Chichester, New York etc. : Wiley.

Teskey, F.N. (1985) *Novel computer architectures for data storage and retrieval.* London : British Library Research and Development Department report no. 5845.

Tharp, A.L. and Tai, K.C. (1982) The practicality of text signatures for accelerating string searching. Software - Practice and Experience vol. 12 pp. 35-44.

Vickery, A. and Brooks, H.M. (1987a) Expert systems and their applications in library and information systems. Online Review vol. 11, pp. 149-165.

Vickery, A. and Brooks, H.M. (1987b) PLEXUS the expert system for referral. Information Processing and Management vol. 23, pp. 99-117.

Vickery, A. Brooks, H.M. Robinson, B. and Vickery, B. (1987) A reference and referral system using expert system techniques. Journal of Documentation vol. 43, pp. 1-23.

Wade, S.J. and Willett, P. (1988) INSTRUCT: a teaching package for experimental methods in information retrieval. Part 3. Browsing, clustering and query expansion. Program vol. 22, pp. 44-61.

Wade, S.J. Willett, P., Robinson, B., Vickery, A. and Vickery, B. (1988) A comparison of knowledge-based and statistically-based techniques for reference retrieval. Online Review vol. 12, pp. 91-108.

Walker, P. (1985) The Transputer. Byte vol. 10(5) pp. 219-235.

Weide, B. (1977) A survey of analysis techniques for discrete algorithms. Computing Surveys vol. 9, pp. 291-313.

Willett, P. *(ed.)* (1988) *Document retrieval systems.* London: Taylor Graham.

Zeng Min-zu, (1987) Progress towards systemization of Chinese information processing in BDS. *International symposium on developing strategy of computer-based Chinese data processing, 1987, NLC, Beijing.*

Index

Software Index

General index

The authors

Dr John Ashford is the Managing Director of a specialist consultancy firm, Ashford Associates Limited, based in Maidenhead, UK

Dr Peter Willett is a Reader in Information Science in the Department of Information Studies, University of Sheffield, UK

More details . . . .

Peter Willett is Reader in Information Science in the Department of Information Studies, University of Sheffield. Following a first degree in Chemistry at Exeter College, Oxford, Dr Willett came to Sheffield in 1975 to study for an MSc in Information Science. This was followed by doctoral and post-doctoral research before he was awarded a Lectureship in Information Science in 1979. He became a Senior Lecturer in 1986 and Reader in 1988. He is a Member of the Institute of Information Scientists and of the British Computer Society, of which he is currently the chairman of the Information Retrieval Specialist Group.

Peter Willett's research interests are in the use of computer techniques for the storage and retrieval of information in databases of text and of chemical structures. His doctoral research involved the development of techniques for the automatic indexing of databases of chemical reactions and this work has now been implemented in several commercial chemical software packages. He then began work on the use of automatic classification, or cluster analysis, methods for the organisation of document databases and has subsequently extended this work to the organisation of files of chemical structures, such as those used in the fine chemicals industry. He now heads a research group which is currently involved with the development of non-Boolean searching techniques for text databases; chemical structure-property correlation techniques for drug discovery programmes; the processing of 3-D representations of molecular structure; and the use of parallel computer hardware for a wide range of applications in the general area of information retrieval.

John Ashford studied geology at the University of Glasgow, and did research on volcanic complexes and then on steel-making refractories. Early contacts first with numerical and then with real-time computing lead to a decade spent in the use of operational research and computing techniques in industrial applications, particularly steelmaking and high volume light engineering. Experience with a major publisher revealed the potential for the use of computers in handling textual information, and he has worked mainly in related fields since. Dr Ashford is a Fellow of the Geological Society of London, and also of the Institute of Information Scientists.

From 1970 to 1974 he was responsible for setting up the management science and computer services division of a diversified market research group, and during this time published early designs for integrated minicomputer based library systems, and developed the structured interactive data entry processes used in the first major retrospective conversions of bibliographic databases in the United Kingdom, for LASER and for the British National Bibliography.

Ashford Associates Limited was formed in 1974 to offer design and consultancy services in library automation independent of vendors of computers or of software. Since then, interest has broadened from library automation as the central concern, to include the design and development of large scale text retrieval systems; strategic planning of the information system needs of legislative assemblies; text databases for publishers and latterly electronic publishing generally; geographic information systems; and studies of the document storage and retrieval infrastructures needed in large scale engineering drawings management and office automation systems.

Projects have been undertaken for clients in Australia, Finland, France, Holland, Hong Kong, Portugal, the United Kingdom, the United States of America and elsewhere, for several major oil companies, for government departments, for research establishments, public and many special libraries, and for several of the suppliers of information retrieval and library automation package software. In September 1986, John Ashford was awarded the ISI prize for the best paper in the Journal of Information Science in 1985.

Computing Books from Chartwell-Bratt

GENERAL COMPUTING BOOKS

Compiler Physiology for Beginners, M Farmer, 279pp, ISBN 0-86238-064-2
Dictionary of Computer and Information Technology, D Lynch, 225 pages, ISBN 0-86238-128-2
File Structure and Design, M Cunningham, 211pp, ISBN 0-86238-065-0
Information Technology Dictionary of Acronyms and Abbreviations, D Lynch, 270pp, ISBN 0-86238-153-3
The IBM Personal Computer with BASIC and PC-DOS, B Kynning, 320pp, ISBN 0-86238-080-4

PROGRAMMING LANGUAGES

An Intro to LISP, P Smith, 130pp, ISBN 0-86238-187-8
An Intro to OCCAM 2 Programming, Bowler, *et al,* 109pp, ISBN 0-86238-137-1
Cobol for Mainframe and Micro, D Watson, 177pp, ISBN 0-86238-082-0
Comparative Languages: 2nd Ed, J R Malone, 125pp, ISBN 0-86238-123-1
Fortran 77 for Non-Scientists, P Adman, 109pp, ISBN 0-86238-074-X
Fortran 77 Solutions to Non-Scientific Problems, P Adman, 150pp, ISBN 0-86238-087-1
Fortran Lectures at Oxford, F Pettit, 135pp, ISBN 0-86238-122-3
LISP: From Foundations to Applications, G Doukidis *et al,* 228pp, ISBN 0-86238-191-6
Programming Language Semantics, C Rattray, 135pp, ISBN 0-86238-066-9
Simula Begin, G M Birtwistle *et al,* 391pp, ISBN 0-86238-009-X
The Intensive C Course: 2nd Edition, M Farmer, 167pp, ISBN 0-86238-114-2
The Intensive Pascal Course, M Farmer, 111pp, ISBN 0-86238-063-4

ASSEMBLY LANGUAGE PROGRAMMING

Coding the 68000, N Hellawell, 214pp, ISBN 0-86238-180-0
Computer Organisation and Assembly Language Programming, L Ohlsson & P Stenstrom, 128pp, ISBN 0-86238-129-0
What is machine code and what can you do with it? N Hellawell, 104pp, ISBN 0-86238-132-0

PROGRAMMING TECHNIQUES

Discrete-events simulations models in PASCAL/MT+ on a microcomputer, L P Jennergren, 135pp, ISBN 0-86238-053-7
Information and Coding, J A Llewellyn, 152pp, ISBN 0-86238-099-5
JSP - A Practical Method of Program Design, L Ingevaldsson, 204pp, ISBN 0-86238-107-X
JSD - Method for System Development, L Ingevaldsson, 248pp, ISBN 0-86238-103-7
Linear Programming: A Computational Approach: 2nd Ed, K K Lau, 150pp, ISBN 0-86238-182-7

Programming for Beginners: the structured way, D Bell & P Scott, 178pp, ISBN 0-86238-130-4

Software Engineering for Students, M Coleman & S Pratt, 195pp, ISBN 0-86238-115-0

Software Taming with Dimensional Design, M Coleman & S Pratt, 164pp, ISBN 0-86238-142-8

Systems Programming with JSP, B Sanden, 186pp, ISBN 0-86238-054-5

MATHEMATICS AND COMPUTING

Fourier Transforms in Action, F Pettit, 133pp, ISBN 0-86238-088-X

Generalised Coordinates, L G Chambers, 90pp, ISBN 0-86238-079-0

Statistics and Operations Research, I P Schagen, 300pp, ISBN 0-86238-077-4

Teaching of Modern Engineering Mathematics, L Rade (ed), 225pp, ISBN 0-86238-173-8

Teaching of Statistics in the Computer Age, L Rade (ed), 248pp, ISBN 0-86238-090-1

The Essentials of Numerical Computation, M Bartholomew-Biggs, 241pp, ISBN 0-86238-029-4

DATABASES AND MODELLING

Database Analysis and Design, H Robinson, 378pp, ISBN 0-86238-018-9

Databases and Database Systems, E Oxborrow, 256pp, ISBN 0-86238-091-X

Data Bases and Data Models, B Sundgren, 134pp, ISBN 0-86238-031-6

Towards Transparent Databases, G Sandstrom, 192pp, ISBN 0-86238-095-2

Information Modelling, J Bubenko (ed), 687pp, ISBN 0-86238-006-5

UNIX

An Intro to the Unix Operating System, C Duffy, 152pp, ISBN 0-86238-143-6

Operating Systems through Unix, G Emery, 96pp, ISBN 0-86238-086-3

SYSTEMS ANALYSIS AND DEVELOPMENT

Systems Analysis and Development: 2nd Ed, P Layzell & P Loucopoulos, 232pp, ISBN 0-86238-156-8

SYSTEMS DESIGN

Computer Systems: Where Hardware meets Software, C Machin, 200pp, ISBN 0-86238-075-8

Distributed Applications and Online Dialogues: a design method for application systems, A Rasmussen, 271pp, ISBN 0-86238-105-3

HARDWARE

Computers from First Principles, M Brown, 128pp, ISBN 0-86238-027-8

Fundamentals of Microprocessor Systems, P Witting, 525pp, ISBN 0-86238-030-8

NETWORKS

Communication Network Protocols: 2nd Ed, B Marsden, 345pp, ISBN 0-86238-106-1
Computer Networks: Fundamentals and Practice, M D Bacon *et al,* 109pp, ISBN 0-86238-028-6
Datacommunication: Data Networks, Protocols and Design, L Ewald & E Westman, 350pp, ISBN 0-86238-092-8
Telecommunications: Telephone Networks 1, Ericsson & Televerket, 147pp, ISBN 0-86238-093-6
Telecommunications: Telephone Networks 2, Ericsson & Televerket, 176pp, ISBN 0-86238-113-4

GRAPHICS

An Introductory Course in Computer Graphics, R Kingslake, 146pp, ISBN 0-86238-073-1
Techniques of Interactive Computer Graphics, A Boyd, 242pp, ISBN 0-86238-024-3
Two-dimensional Computer Graphics, S Laflin, 85pp, ISBN 0-86238-127-4

APPLICATIONS

Computers in Health and Fitness, J Abas, 106pp, ISBN 0-86238-155-X
Developing Expert Systems, G Doukidis, E Whitley, ISBN 0-86238-196-7
Expert Systems Introduced, D Daly, 180pp, ISBN 0-86238-185-1
Handbook of Finite Element Software, J Mackerle & B Fredriksson, approx 1000pp, ISBN 0-86238-135-5
Inside **Data Processing: computers and their effective use in business,** A deWatteville, 150pp, ISBN 0-86238-181-9
Proceedings of the Third Scandinavian Conference on Image Analysis, P Johansen & P Becker (eds) 426pp, ISBN 0-86238-039-1
Programmable Control Systems, G Johannesson, 136pp, ISBN 0-86238-046-4
Risk and Reliability Appraisal on Microcomputers, G Singh, with G Kiangi, 142pp, ISBN 0-86238-159-2
Statistics with Lotus 1-2-3, M Lee & J Soper, 207pp, ISBN 0-86238-131-2

HCI

Human/Computer Interaction: from voltage to knowledge, J Kirakowski, 250pp, ISBN 0-86238-179-7
Information Ergonomics, T Ivegard, 228pp, ISBN 0-86238-032-4
Computer Display Designer's Handbook, E Wagner, approx 300pp, ISBN 0-86238-171-1

INFORMATION AND SOCIETY

Access to Government Records: International Perspectives and Trends, T Riley, 112pp, ISBN 0-86238-119-3
CAL/CBT - the great debate, D Marshall, 300pp, ISBN 0-86238-144-4

Economic and Trade-Related Aspects of Transborder Dataflow,
R Wellington-Brown, 93pp, ISBN 0-86238-110-X
Information Technology and a New International Order, J Becker, 141pp, ISBN
0-86238-043-X
People or Computers: Three Ways of Looking at Information Systems,
M Nurminen, 1218pp, ISBN 0-86238-184-3
Transnational Data Flows in the Information Age, C Hamelink, 115pp, ISBN
0-86238-042-1

SCIENCE HANDBOOKS

Alpha Maths Handbook, L Rade, 199pp, ISBN 0-86238-036-7
Beta Maths Handbook, L Rade, 425pp, ISBN 0-86238-140-1
Handbook of Electronics, J de Sousa Pires, approx 750pp, ISBN 0-86238-061-8
Nuclear Analytical Chemistry, D Brune *et al,* 557pp, ISBN 0-86238-047-2
Physics Handbook, C Nordling & J Osterman, 430pp, ISBN 0-86238-037-5
The V-Belt Handbook, H Palmgren, 287pp, ISBN 0-86238-111-8

Chartwell-Bratt specialise in excellent books at affordable prices.

For further details contact your local bookshop, or ring Chartwell-Bratt direct on
01-467 1956 (Access/Visa welcome.)

Ring or write for our *free* catalogue.

Chartwell-Bratt (Publishing & Training) Ltd, Old Orchard, Bickley Road,
Bromley, Kent, BR1 2NE, United Kingdom.
Tel 01-467 1956, Fax 01-467 1754, Telecom Gold 84:KJM001,
Telex 9312100451(CB)